THE
DIVERSI
OF
SCRIPTURE

OVERTURES TO BIBLICAL THEOLOGY

A series of studies in biblical theology designed to explore fresh dimensions of research and to suggest ways in which the biblical heritage may address contemporary culture

Editors

WALTER BRUEGGEMANN, Dean of Academic Affairs and Professor of Old Testament at Eden Theological Seminary

JOHN R. DONAHUE, S.J., Associate Professor of New Testament at Vanderbilt Divinity School

A
Theological
Interpretation

THE
DIVERSITY
OF
SCRIPTURE

PAUL D. HANSON

F FORTRESS PRESS   Philadelphia

To

Russell Samuel Rosenberger

Betsy Ross Rosenberger

Library of Congress Cataloging in Publication Data

Hanson, Paul D.
  The Diversity of Scripture

  (Overtures to Biblical Theology ; 11)
  Bibliography: p.
  Includes index.
  1. Bible—Theology.   1. Title.   II. Series.
  BS543.H35   230   81–43079
  ISBN 0–8006–1535–2   AACR2

9014K81   Printed in the United States of America   1–1535

Contents

v

Series Foreword

Biblical theology has been a significant part of modern study of the Jewish and Christian Scriptures. Prior to the ascendancy of historical criticism of the Bible in the nineteenth century, biblical theology was subordinated to the dogmatic concerns of the churches, and the Bible too often provided a storehouse of rigid proof texts. When biblical theology was cut loose from its moorings to dogmatic theology to become an enterprise seeking its own methods and categories, attention was directed to what the Bible itself had to say. A dogmatic concern was replaced by an historical one so that biblical theology was understood as an investigation of what was believed by different communities in different situations. By the end of the nineteenth century biblical theology was virtually equated with the history of the religion of the authors who produced biblical documents or of the communities which used them.

While these earlier perspectives have become more refined and sophisticated, they still describe the parameters of what is done in the name of biblical theology—moving somewhere between the normative statements of dogmatic theology and the descriptive concerns of the history of religions. Th. Vriezen, in his *An Outline of Old Testament Theology* (Dutch, 1949; ET, 1958), sought to combine these concerns by devoting the first half of his book to historical considerations and the second half to theological themes. But even that effort did not break out of the stalemate of categories. In more recent times Old Testament theology has been dominated by two paradigmatic works. In his *Theology of the Old Testament* (German, 1933–39; ET, 1967) W. Eichrodt has provided a comprehensive statement around fixed categories which reflect classical dogmatic interests, although the centrality of covenant in

ix

his work reflects the Bible's own categories. By contrast, G. von Rad in his *Old Testament Theology* (German, 1960; ET, 1965) has presented a study of theological traditions with a primary concern for the historical dynamism of the traditions. In the case of New Testament theology, historical and theological concerns are rather roughly juxtaposed in the work of A. Richardson, *An Introduction to the Theology of the New Testament*. As in the case of the Old Testament, there are two major options or presentations which dominate in New Testament studies. The history-of-religion school has left its mark on the magisterial work of R. Bultmann, who proceeds from an explanation of the expressions of faith of the earliest communities and their theologians to a statement of how their understanding of existence under faith speaks to us today. The works of O. Cullmann and W. G. Kümmel are clear New Testament statements of *Heilsgeschichte* under the aegis of the tension between promise and fulfillment—categories reminiscent of von Rad.

As recently as 1962 K. Stendahl again underscored the tension between historical description and normative meaning by assigning to the biblical theologian the task of describing what the Bible *meant*, not what it *means* or *how* it can have meaning. However, this objectivity of historical description is too often found to be a mirror of the observer's hidden preunderstanding, and the adequacy of historical description is contingent on one generation's discoveries and postulates. Also, the yearning and expectation of believers and would-be believers will not let biblical theology rest with the descriptive task alone. The growing strength of Evangelical Protestantism and the expanding phenomenon of charismatic Catholicism are but vocal reminders that people seek in the Bible a source of alternative value systems. By its own character and by the place it occupies in our culture, the Bible will not rest easy as merely an historical artifact.

Thus it seems a fitting time to make "overtures" concerning biblical theology. It is not a time for massive tomes which claim too much. It appears not even to be a time for firm conclusions which are too comprehensive. It is a time for pursuit of fresh hints, for exploration of new intuitions which may reach beyond old conclusions, set categories, and conventional methods. The books in this series are concerned not only with what is seen and heard, with what the Bible said, but also with what the Bible says and the ways in which seeing and hearing are done.

In putting forth these *Overtures* much remains unsettled. The certainties of the older biblical theology *in service* of dogmatics, as well as of the more recent biblical theology movement *in lieu* of dogmatics, are no longer present. Nor is there on the scene anyone of the stature of a von Rad or a Bultmann to offer a synthesis which commands the theological engagement of a generation and summons the church to a new restatement of the biblical message. In a period characterized by an information explosion, the relation of analytic study to attempts at synthesis is unsettled. Also unsettled is the question whether the scholarly canon of the university or the passion of the confessing community provides a language and idiom of discourse, and equally unsettled—and unsettling—is the question whether biblical theology is simply one more specialization in an already fragmented study of Scripture or whether it is finally the point of it all.

But much remains clear. Not simply must the community of biblical scholars address fresh issues and articulate new categories for the well-being of our common professional task; equally urgent is the fact that the dominant intellectual tradition of the West seems now to carry less conviction and to satisfy only weakly the new measures of knowing which are among us. We do not know exactly what role the Bible will play in new theological statements or religious postures, nor what questions the Bible can and will address, but *Overtures* will provide a locus where soundings may be taken.

We not only intend that *Overtures* should make contact with people professionally involved in biblical studies, but hope that the series will speak to all who care about the heritage of the biblical tradition. We hope that the volumes will represent the best in a literary and historical study of biblical traditions without canonizing historical archaism. We hope also that the studies will be relevant without losing the mystery of biblical religion's historical distance, and that the studies touch on significant themes, motifs, and symbols of the Bible without losing the rich diversity of the biblical tradition. It is a time for normative literature which is not heavy-handed, but which seriously challenges not only our conclusions, but also the shape of our questions.

Paul D. Hanson, distinguished young Old Testament scholar at Harvard, has already hinted at an emerging new paradigm for the doing of biblical theology. In his programmatic book *The Dawn of Apocalyptic* (Fortress Press, 1975) he has explored the ongoing tension in the Old Testament between "visionaries" and "pragmatists." In a more recent study, *Dynamic Transcendence* (Fortress Press, 1978), he has recast the same argument in more contemporary categories, aimed at current hermeneutical issues. There he speaks of the tension between "teleological" and "cosmic" perspectives. In the present volume, Hanson continues to develop these pairs, both to describe substantive matters in the text itself and as interpretive angles for our present work.

Hanson's book is in the end a statement about the authority of the Bible for the believing community. He reacts critically and negatively against every effort to reduce the Bible to a single statement, dogmatic, philosophical, or psychological. Faithful interpretation must recognize and deal with the undoubted diversity and recognize that different theological claims are present in different texts. The only way the Bible can be a perennially authoritative word is in being free and dynamic enough to address different situations differently. Thus, "to be . . . authentically human means different things in different circumstances" (p. 58). And one may extrapolate from Hanson that to be faithful to God means different things in different circumstances.

Of course the differences and diversity to which Hanson points are not random or undisciplined. He understands the differences to be orderly and moving along a purposeful continuum. It is within the broad trajectory of God's ongoing governance that the different traditions must be studied to discern the meaning of Scripture. Hanson is singularly adept at constructing dialectical categories which are necessary to describe the fullness of biblical faith. Fundamental to his thinking is his earlier construct, "pragmatic/visionary." Because his earlier study was concerned with apocalyptic, his book tilted to an appreciation of that polarity. Here Hanson seeks to balance the reforming zeal of the prophets with the human need for structure in personal and communal life. In this effort he interprets the royal tradition as an essential response to anomie. Thus Hanson affirms the tradition of "form" even in tension with the tradition of "reform." But because Hanson is sociologically sensitive, he also sees that the royal tendency is potentially reactionary and oppressive. The book leaves the matter open. That unresolved issue (that is, how to assess the traditions) indicates that more work needs to be done in terms of such a dynamic. And Hanson offers his work only as a step into new perspectives.

A byproduct of Hanson's mode of interpretation is attention to the vitality and creativity of language. It is that sensitivity to language that keeps the constructs fresh and dynamic. And it is that same sensitivity that keeps the constructs from becoming empty forms.

Hanson is attentive to the interface of sociology and faith and, therefore, to the interaction of tradition and community. This book is a part of his process of securing a new method that deals responsibly with the confessional character of the material. Thus the main issues are stated with reference not only to the text, but also to the contemporary responsibilities and possibilities of the interpreting community. Hanson offers a genuine *Overture* for a method that refuses to leave the interpreting community outside the scope of critical method.

WALTER BRUEGGEMANN
JOHN R. DONAHUE, S.J.

Preface

In mid-March, as I was writing the final chapter of this book, I received a note from one of my students. Enclosed was an article which she had come across "while thumbing through various periodicals here at Mother's," that is, at her home in Michigan. After chapel the previous Wednesday, I had discussed with her an issue which had weighed heavily on my mind. Now in the letter she explained that she hoped the article would help me see the matter from a biblical perspective. It did.

Her note ended with this sentence: "I won't document the article's source or you might not read it!" It was obviously from a periodical reflecting a view of the Bible of which I had been critical in classes.

I draw attention to this incident for this reason: the ideas in this book are directed toward fellow Christians of many different perspectives. The book is intended to stimulate the kind of dialogue, sharing, and criticism from which we all learn. Diversity of the fruitful sort which keeps faith open to the living God is not found only in the Bible. It is a rich part of contemporary church life. But we have much to learn about a style of dialogue which will balance commitment with openness and growth.

Within the context of Christian dialogue I want to offer a positive theological assessment of diversity in the Bible. Precisely from a theological point of view, the significance of diversity is profound. It bespeaks nothing less important than the biblical view that the God of Israel is a God who is encountered in the stuff of history and human experience. If biblical narratives and teachings were derived from a timeless myth or a rigid religious system, we should expect little theological diversity. But biblical writings are not a series of glosses on a preexistent, primordial text. They are responses to a relationship with God which is experienced as ongoing. And they are born of the desire to re-spond faithfully within each new chapter of that relationship's unfolding.

This is not to deny that the faith of the Christian is a unified faith. But the Source of that unity must not be misplaced. The believer's faith is one because God is one. At the same time, the cloud of witnesses which nurtures that faith and keeps it open and growing is rich in its diversity. Diversity is a most natural part of a faith relating to the one true God. For God is a God of holy mystery, and a God active in all time and space in living relations with growing communities and individuals. As students of the Bible, we express faithfulness to our scriptural heritage not through hasty harmonization or codification of the diverse witnesses into rigid dogmatic formulations, but by understanding each witness in its distinctiveness. To appreciate the diversity is to keep the faith of the church fresh and growing. It is to keep faith grounded in its only true Source rather than in the vehicles through which the saints of the ages have sought to point toward that one true Source. Krister Stendahl, on reading the first draft of this book, glossed this thought with one of the pithy similes which have characterized his teaching and writing for years: like good vegetable soup, where you look not for mush but for each vegetable contributing its distinctive flavor, the Bible should be pre-sented with each of its parts kept fresh and alive.

Such a position accords well with the biblical doctrine of God as Reality beyond human image or formulation. No one human confession is capable of capturing the total mystery. The rich diversity of confes-sions which we have in the Bible is the most adequate means for opening ourselves to as much of the divine mystery as possible. This openness to a rich diversity in turn conditions the contemporary community to be open to God's presence in events and experiences of our own day. The present book, therefore, explores ways in which we can appropriate the whole testimony of Scripture, be open to the one true God, and be drawn into God's ongoing creative, redemptive purpose by stretching our imaginations to encompass a biblical heritage which is rich and diverse.

We call Scripture "God's Word," thereby expressing the conviction that in these writings God spoke to ancient Jews and Christians *and* speaks to us. But between "them" and "us" lies a considerable gap. The languages in which the messages were written are not our languages. The thought worlds are not ours either. We are able to reconstruct only im-perfectly the cultural, political, and social settings within which those messages were received and interpreted. How then can we move at all from the historical theological confession that "in these writings God spoke to ancient Jews and Christians" to the contemporary theological confession that "in these same writings God speaks to us"? Such a move obviously is predicated on several presuppositions of faith. These presuppositions can be summarized briefly: Within the events and through the confessions of biblical times, God was revealing a universal purpose. Moreover, God has continued to reveal that purpose down to the present. And while a huge gap in time and ways of human thought cannot be denied, the central dynamic of the Bible has had an unbroken mediator in the confessional heritage. Within the life of worship and service of the church, we are addressed by that central dynamic and are enabled to interpret it and relate it to the present world.

Accepting these presuppositions as a part of a critically informed faith, we go to Scripture expectantly, open to tutoring in God's ways in our world, and in the ways we can be God's people. This is not a mindless task, as if we needed only to memorize symbols, formulas, and ancient languages. Amid those symbols, formulas, and languages a faithful way of understanding and living is unfolding, and the challenge facing us is not to prove our ability to memorize, but to accept graciously a call to be drawn into that way of understanding and living. As we begin to grasp that way, we express it not in archaic words and meaningless rituals, but in the words and concepts and actions that enrich and relate to our own experiences. This reformulation occurs through a dialogue within which both the ancient vehicles of expression and our modern vocabularies are enriched, as the penetration of the saints breaks open for us new angles of vision, and as our own experiences cast new light on ancient Scripture.

We enter into this dialogue, then, expectantly, but also playfully.[1] We know that the God addressing us surpasses both scriptural formulations and our own abilities to comprehend, but we also take heart in the knowledge that God graciously draws near to us in both. So we seek to open ourselves to the way of understanding and living which is the way of grace, a way already accomplished and only waiting to be received. We open ourselves to that way out of gratitude, for we desire our response to be fitting and our gratitude to express itself in commitment. After all, we have nothing more with which to express our praise.

Openness to God's Word in Scripture and experience involves risk.

We need only be reminded of the times we convinced ourselves that what we desired was God's will for our lives, only to be awakened by Word or experience to the realization that we were identifying God's will with what our own sinful hearts desired. And not only the new car or house or gem can thus be confused, but also the theological model or doctrine or symbol. Though cautious and repentant, however, we do not despair, if we allow ourselves to be guided by the thirty-five-hundred year trajectory of divine purpose coming to us through our confessional heritage, and if we cling to the master paradigm of our faith, Jesus Christ, in whom God's purpose broke into our world with uncommon clarity.

The basic ideas relating to the polarities of faith discussed in this book were first presented in lecture form at the following institutions and conferences: Saint Mary's University, Halifax; Trinity Seminary, Columbus; The University of Missouri, Columbia; Union Theological Seminary in Virginia, Richmond; and the Rocky Mountain District of the American Lutheran Church. I am indebted to those who extended the invitations, and to those who responded with comments and criticisms.

As I draw inspiration from examples of faith lived warmly and stead-fastly, I look especially to Professor and Mrs. Russell S. Rosenberger of Gettysburg, Pennsylvania, whom, thanks to my marriage to their daughter Cynthia, I can proudly call Mom and Dad. In dedicating this book to them, I gratefully acknowledge the model of the faithful response which they have given to our family and to many, many others.

Cambridge, Massachusetts   P. D. H.
April 1980

CHAPTER 1

The Bible

The Language
of a Living Relationship

THE LANGUAGE OF CONFESSION

An expression of love need not ascend to the aesthetic heights of an Elizabethan sonnet to address the heart of the beloved. Words stammered by lips groping for a way to share the feelings of a full heart constitute a language with a power of its own. This is the language of confession. And the verification principle which applies to it is not that of the scientific laboratory, where the criteria of consistency and facticity reign. Truthfulness, fittingness, genuineness, faithfulness of response—such are the qualities of confession.

By way of example, a husband does not retain in his memory the statements with which his wife expresses her love in order to check them for consistency. Picture husband and wife enjoying their first quiet moments of the day together, having just got their children to bed. She embraces him and whispers, "I am the luckiest woman in the world, to have a family like ours." Astonishing thing it would be if he were to tear himself away and snap back in indignation, "But just a week ago you claimed that you were the luckiest woman in the world, to be married to *me!*" In the function of such words, consistency is not the main objective. Rather, the honest, faithful expression of true feelings within the trust and freedom of a living relationship is involved, and a rich diversity of expressions is but a sign of the newness of love.

Equally astonishing would be another response: "Before I shall believe you, you must prove to me that there is not a luckier woman in the world, somewhere!" Here the honesty and faithfulness of the expression is lost by introduction of the alien criterion of facticity.

If in life's intimate and abiding relationships the rigid application of

1

the criteria of consistency and facticity obscure the meaning of words, is the same not true of those words which address us as God's Word and which draw us into the most intimate and abiding relationship of all? Yet for centuries many Christians have not heard God's Word addressing them within a living relationship. Getting in the way has been the notion that a test of true faith is belief in the internal formal consistency of all teachings within the Bible and the facticity of all biblical statements. As the focus of attention turns to harmonizing and proving inerrancy, a rich collection of confessions arising from various stages in a long, living relationship between God and people fossilizes into factual reports and infallible doctrines. The Bible ceases to be a witness to the life of fellowship with the living God and becomes a collection of reports and teachings which yields a body of doctrine regarded as the contents of true faith.

The history of biblical interpretation is not lacking in voices protesting this transformation, and the Spinozas and Wellhausens will be remembered for their honest attempts to let the Bible speak for itself. But too often the debate has been forced outside the community of faith, in part because of the rigidity of orthodox leaders, in part because of the arrogance of critical scholars. Promising insights have become the weapons of outside attack on church and synagogue.

We stand in agreement with those biblical scholars who sought to free the Bible from the straitjacket of dogmatic systems. Now, thanks to the climate of open theological inquiry that prevails in some denominations today, we are able to carry on the kind of scholarship which seeks to let the Bible speak on its own terms *within* the context of the church. This we do with great joy, for we find that our commitment to the church is implied within our commitment to a biblically based faith.

We glimpse an exciting prospect here, of Christians from various confessions joining together in the exploration of Scripture, experiencing a freedom from aggressiveness or defensiveness because of their sense of common dedication to a divine purpose revealed in the Bible, a purpose which transcends the interests of any individual group or person. In this Scripture, we are addressed by God within a relationship that is living and forward-moving, and we receive a vision of the unfolding of God's plan from the confessions of many witnesses in the Bible. It is no more appropriate for us to apply rigid criteria of consistency and facticity to these confessions than it would be for a husband to apply such criteria to his wife's confessions of love. For the primary objective of biblical study is not a consistent system of doctrine but as full a sense of the presence and purpose of God as possible. Fortunately in the Bible we find fullness both in quantity and in diversity, for a vast chorus of the faithful gives expression to God's initiative. They have done so from many different perspectives, from widely disparate points in space and time, and in a multitude of literary forms. Their confessions are unified by one fact alone: they all respond to the creative, redemptive activity of the one true God.

In a most basic theological sense, consistency and facticity construed rigidly are unthinkable within a collection of writings bearing witness to God's living relationship with a people. How could any one confession capture the fullness of the holy and ineffable God? Or how could widely diverse confessional responses to the *mysterium divinum* duplicate one another and yield one simple picture? Throughout biblical history, God, in God's sovereignty, has acted to create, redeem, judge, and sustain, and recipients of God's grace have responded. How much richer and more profound is our knowledge of God because of the diversity of expression which has grown out of the long history of this living relationship. We must seek to capture the meaning of this witness to God's grace with the same freedom and humility as characterized the biblical writers—freedom from anxiety about *the* definitive and consistent statement, and humility as regards the human capacity to describe adequately the holy God. For it is idolatrous to claim that any human formulation can definitively describe the one true God. The fitting way for believers to express their gratitude and describe their experience of God's presence and purpose therefore can be learned from the Bible. For there we find richly diverse confessions which seek to give faithful response to God's grace, which unabashedly combine objective observations with subjective interpretations, and which above all freely express an ardor that refuses to be inhibited by rigid notions of consistency and facticity. Puny indeed is the faith which constricts the richness of biblical traditions and confessions to fit into a dogmatic structure. A living faith, by contrast, opens up to embrace every authentic witness to God's presence and activity, and it is stretched in the process to ever-heightened reverence and perceptivity.

We are not commending a mindless or purely sentimental response to the confessions and traditions of the Bible. Indeed, every chapter of the present book will address ways in which the diversity of the biblical witness can be interpreted. But at the outset we are pleading for an openness to the total address of Scripture, lest we select only what reinforces our present views and exclude the possibility of growth. Once open to the rich diversity of the Bible, we shall see that it is not a collection of disconnected statements. Rather, a common focus on the one true God is apparent—a God whose purpose over all centuries has been steadfast. This will invite us to discern patterns within the rich diversity of the Bible, patterns which reveal important polarities that mark out the field of tension within which God's plan for creation has unfolded in the consciousness of the community of faith.[1] We shall see how these polarities both deepen our understanding of God's purpose and invite connections with corresponding polarities that are discernible within the experiences of our own modern existence. Diversity in the Bible is therefore interpreted neither as a sign of arbitrariness nor as a sign of fragmentation on the most basic level of reality. It is seen as the natural result of the one true God's graciously relating to humans, drawing humans into a relationship inviting free response and full engagement.

It has been argued, however, that adherence to a doctrine of inerrancy alone keeps the church faithful to the classical Christian position.[2] This argument overlooks the rich diversity which is found also in the realm of biblical interpretation over the course of the history of the church. One need only think of the freedom with which medieval interpreters sought the spiritual meaning of the text that lay beneath the literal sense, or consider Luther's critical comments regarding the Books of James and Revelation. It is true, however, that over the major span of church history, consistency and facticity were not the problems they are for us today.[3] The Bible could be interpreted quite literally as a factual description, whether or not one then proceeded to search for a deeper meaning underlying the surface. Accordingly, the essential question which arises today is this: Should the church revert back to a precritical position, as if two centuries of historical research on the Bible did not exist?

There is no way to deny that many Christians find the precritical position appropriate and true. And for those who are unaware or untroubled by problems of literary inconsistencies, factual discrepancies, or theological diversity in the Bible, there is no reason why a traditional approach may not support a life of faith. We are concerned, however, with believers who have fallen heir to questions which arose among eighteenth- and nineteenth-century thinkers, questions relating to the facticity of the biblical narrative and to the contemporary authoritativeness of the world brought to light by a strictly literal reading. Should such questions be repressed? Should they be operative in an intellectual inquiry but divorced from faith? Or should they be dedicated to a deeper probing of the meaning of the Bible in the service of faith? There is little doubt that debate will continue about whether two centuries of critical biblical scholarship have led to a deeper understanding of the meaning of Scripture or to a departure from a true biblical faith, and in such debate decisions will be determined in large measure by presuppositions. The present book addresses those who feel that questions do arise in the interpretation of the contemporary meaning of Scripture which deserve examination and reflection, and that presuppositions, while unavoidable, should themselves be subjected to careful theological examination by the individual believer and the church.

INSIGHTS FROM THE FIELD OF INTERPRETATION THEORY

In the last two centuries, insightful critics have also sought answers for the question about the contemporary meaning of ancient texts. Through their efforts an ancient discipline has been infused with new life: the discipline of hermeneutics, or interpretation theory. Several insights which derive from these modern hermeneutical studies deserve mention here, inasmuch as they promise to contribute to a more adequate understanding of the way in which the Bible can relate to our modern world.

1. First to be considered is an insight addressing the *dimension of subjectivity* in every literary and artistic work as well as in every interpretive effort. In the long history of attempts to defend the inerrancy of the biblical narrative, endless devices, from the comical to the absurd, have been marshaled to deny this dimension of subjectivity. But it has never been exorcised and remains as an embarrassment to defenders of a traditional literalist position. In the writings of Friedrich Schleiermacher and Wilhelm Dilthey, as well as in twentieth-century writers following in their tradition, attempts at denial or rationalization gave way to a very positive evaluation of the subjective dimension. The fact that ancient narratives cannot be read literally only exposes the more significant sides of life which they address by evoking meaningful questions and encouraging serious reflection. Already within their ancient settings the classics functioned to foster a deeper understanding of the world and the place of the self in that world. It is because of this capacity that they were

cherished over the centuries. In the contemporary interpretation of the classics the role of the subjective should not be minimized if the dynamic process of fostering understanding, which is their hallmark, is to be continued.

The most daring formulation of this emphasis on the subjective dimension arose in connection with Schleiermacher's use of the term *divination* to describe the function of interpretation.[4] The aim of interpretation is not merely the reproduction of the original work, but an act of new creation not unlike that engaged in by the original author. While subsequent writers have modified this point somewhat, it is clear that any serious reflection on the theory of interpretation must address the role of the subjective dimension both in the original creation of a work and in the subsequent history of its interpretation.

2. A related theme among hermeneutical theorists of the last two hundred years is the *profound significance attributed to language* in the understanding of reality. For Martin Heidegger, it is in language that the world in which we live comes into being.[5] To gain understanding of life it is important to study the monumental expressions of life which have come down to us from the past. Such expressions (and poetry plays a special role here) are not objects in the hands of the interrogating subject. The Cartesian dichotomy which would claim that the essence of the object can be extracted by the subject if the proper instruments are used is abandoned in favor of a view that sees the text itself as the addressing subject. This is possible because great works of literary art give expression to existence in a manner calling our own views into question, thereby prodding us to look more deeply at life.[6]

3. In the case of hermeneutical theorists like Schleiermacher and Heidegger, it is possible to get the impression that texts address us out of a rather disjointed past. Profound insight into existence is found in a Greek ode, a German lyric, or an English play, and although the historicality of each work is emphasized (in opposition to the idealist's conception of pure spirit coming to expression in such media), the question of historical continuity between the individual works is not asked. This accords poorly with a central biblical view, namely, that our understanding of reality in its many facets did not arise in moments disconnected in time and space, but in an ongoing history of salvation. Events and reports of events fall into the pattern of a chain, the links of which connect one with the other. It is in this area that Hans-Georg Gadamer has made important contributions to hermeneutics in his notion of

reality unfolding over the vast span of tradition and in his related concept of the *merging of horizons,* which takes place as the modern interpreter studies a traditional work. Although Gadamer has been accused of forsaking the radical emphasis on historicality in an alleged rapprochement with Hegel in the notion of the continuous disclosure of reality in the tradition, his analysis of the role of tradition in understanding adds a dimension to contemporary hermeneutical theory which prepares the way for a very fruitful exchange of ideas between general hermeneutics and biblical hermeneutics. To the emphases on the positive role of the subjective in interpretation and on the power of language to evoke understanding, Gadamer has added his emphasis on the *developmental dimension,* which is so essential in interpreting a corpus of writings within which faith discerns the unfolding of divine purpose.[7]

In the past, thoughtful individuals whose historical and critical questions cut them off from a literalist position have frequently been told that their world of beliefs and subsequent values would have to be constructed apart from biblical foundations, which had fallen into ruins beneath them. Hermeneutical theory, applied to the classics of antiquity and used in the contemporary interpretation of these works, has pointed in the direction of a way out of the impasse constructed by the literalism/unbiblical humanism dichotomy. A new understanding of the essential character of the biblical writings begins to emerge when it is recognized that much of the power of Scripture lies in its not being limited to a literal description of an ancient world. Indeed, it is the confessional dimension (which inevitably goes deeper than "objective description") that in the biblical writings fosters discernment of divine presence and purpose within the events of human experience and history. And in this important process of discernment the power of language to evoke understanding is manifested. It is manifested already in the ancient confessional heritage which equipped the community of faith to recognize patterns of purpose in the happenings of their world. And it continues to be manifested in the ability of our entire confessional heritage to equip us to discern God's purposes in our world.

For the believer who both confesses the unique role of the Bible in fostering understanding of reality and discerns the unfolding of divine purpose in the events of the entire span reaching from biblical times to the present, a clear language must be developed for describing the nature of revelatory events, biblical confessions, and patterns of divine purpose in history. In this effort, the insights of the hermeneutical theorists as we have been describing them can be combined with the findings of historical-critical studies in laying the basis for more satisfactory ways of interpreting the contemporary meaning of the Bible.

EVALUATION OF INSIGHTS FROM THE FIELD OF INTERPRETATION THEORY

A principle which applies to every dialogue between biblical studies and another discipline or perspective applies emphatically in relation to the field of general hermeneutics: ideas which enhance understanding of the intrinsic meaning of Scripture should be adopted, while at the same time caution is exercised to avoid forcing biblical views into alien structures of thought. Thus it is not enough, for example, uncritically to import into the realm of scriptural interpretation hermeneutical principles and techniques used by Heidegger in his interpretation of a Greek poem. Rather, principles and techniques must be evolved from within the field of biblical studies itself that will be appropriate to this particular corpus. Point for point, then, even the most arresting insights of general hermeneutics must be evaluated and refined in light of the particular qualities of the biblical writings. Briefly, we shall attempt such an evaluation in regard to the three emphases of modern hermeneutics previously mentioned.

1. To begin with, the emphasis of hermeneutical theorists on the *subjective dimension of interpretation* must be examined closely. In the Bible, as in the subsequent writings of the church, confessional responses to events are clearly genuine human responses, in which the community of faith, as a part of its life in communion with the living God, seeks to grasp the ultimate significance of the happenings around it. As such, confessional responses are cast within the language of the world views of the time in question and are restricted by the conceptual limitations of the responders. To recognize this is not to deny the revelatory capacity of confessions and confessional narratives, but is only to recognize that human language is the vehicle in which the discernment of divine presence in past events has reached us. Especially within a confessional community that takes the incarnation seriously, careful attention must be paid to this human vehicle, lest the particularity and historicality of each biblical confession be lost.

Nevertheless, it must also be acknowledged that some scholars have uncritically applied existentialist presuppositions to biblical interpretation, leading to an inordinate emphasis on the subjective. This obscures another essential characteristic of biblical confessions, namely, their rootedness in real happenings of history. A hermeneutic within which the Bible as addressing subject remains sovereign must find a way to balance the objective and subjective dimensions essential to a proper understanding of divine activity in the Bible.

In a reaction against the overemphasis on the subjective in existentialist interpretation, the pendulum must not be allowed to swing too far in the other direction either, toward what would amount to a form of neopositivism. For while there is neither reason to deny the existence nor to question the importance of objective, historical happenings in the experiences of our biblical ancestors, the events reported in the Bible are not those brute happenings, nor can the latter be reconstructed in precise detail on the basis of those events. The events handed on to us through the confessional writings of the Bible are best understood as a blending of actual happenings with the interpretation of the community of faith, an interpretation made possible by viewing those happenings through the lens of the confessional heritage in the context of the community's life of worship and service of the living God.[8] Precisely because biblical events reach us in a symbiosis of the objective and the subjective are they capable of fostering a deeper understanding of life and world for us today.

2. Only in a special sense, then, can the emphasis of modern hermeneutical theorists on the subjective dimension be adopted by biblical interpreters. In a similar fashion, the *emphasis on language* as that which evokes understanding must be enlarged to make room for discernment of divine manifestation not only in Word, but in world, that is, in patterns of order and purpose in nature and history. There is no cause to deny that the concept of divine Word, as it is developed especially in the Deuteronomistic writings and in most of the prophetic books, fits well with the modern emphasis on the evocative power of language. For it describes a Word which breaks into the consciousness of the prophet and shapes the direction of events, directing them toward the fulfillment of divine promises. But other important concepts within the Bible do not fit into a narrowly conceived Word theology. Certainly traditions dealing with God's creation of the world (aside from the P account), with God's mighty acts of deliverance and judgment in history, and with the Almighty's awesome acts in the end-time, necessitate an understanding of divine reality which is more inclusive than language event. Here too, modification and refinement of hermeneutical insights are called for,

as one recognizes a lively interplay between Word and other modes of divine activity.

3. While of great significance in any serious reformulation of biblical interpretation, even Gadamer's *emphasis on the role of tradition* in hermeneutics must be evaluated in relation to the specific characteristics of the biblical writings. This point can be illustrated vividly in light of the findings which have emerged through application of traditio-historical methods of study. By studying the growth of traditions in the Bible, this approach has uncovered, in most historical periods, multiple streams of tradition giving expression to divergent interpretations of events and of God's relationship to those events. In the first instance, therefore, the Bible does not present the community of faith with one rectilinear stream of tradition spanning the centuries. One cannot hope for an immediate merging of ancient with contemporary horizons. That is to say, since a diversity of traditions can often be recognized in one biblical period, simple hermeneutical appropriation is not possible. Rather, the particular characteristics of each stream of tradition must be determined, and the relationship between divergent streams must be studied. Gadamer's emphasis on the role of tradition in interpretation, like the other insights of general hermeneutics, must be applied to biblical interpretation in a special way. Biblical tradition is a complex phenomenon. The theological significance of this complexity must be determined before one can expect merging of horizons—the aim of the interpretive process.

THE THEOLOGICAL SIGNIFICANCE OF DIVERSITY IN THE BIBLE

The diversity of biblical tradition, like the subjective dimension in every biblical confession, can be regarded either as a stumbling block in the way of the Bible's contributing to contemporary understanding or as a great opportunity and challenge. What are we to do with a scriptural corpus which accommodates itself neither to the scheme of the unfolding of pure Spirit nor to the notion of one tradition bearing witness to a simple, unified world view which the church can directly adopt as its own? Some biblical scholars would leave the matter at this point by simply acknowledging the diversity and allowing others to trouble themselves with the alternative ways of dealing with this phenomenon, whether by harmonizing differences so as to create the appearance of unity, by adopting one tradition as normative at the cost of others, or by abandoning entirely the idea of an overall, meaningful witness in the

Bible to reality. But for biblical scholarship to drop the phenomenon after describing the diversity is to leave a job half done, for the Bible itself contains the most lucid illustrations we possess of the manner in which the diversity in tradition can foster an understanding of reality and the ultimate grounding of reality in God which, far from threatening to undermine faith in the God of the Bible, actually fosters a more profound understanding of the activities of that God in the world. Because the theological significance of diversity in biblical tradition has not been given the positive assessment it deserves, the present study focuses especially on this phenomenon. The other two contributions of general hermeneutics, the emphasis on the positive significance of the subjective dimension and on the world-constructing power of language, will certainly enrich our discussion. But at center stage will be the question of the confessional heritage, or tradition—that dynamic stream, with its crosscurrents and eddies, which spans the centuries and offers hope for the merging of the insights and disclosures of antiquity with possibilities for deeper understandings in our own world.

It must be admitted that, in the first instance, we are confronted with a higher degree of complexity than is found in the traditional or even the neoorthodox views of the Bible. We have noted how critical questions have cast doubts on the literalism of the former. Neoorthodoxy acknowledged that historical-critical studies had undermined an ostensive, referential view, but it embraced the notion of an inner history which bridged the gap from biblical times to the present. In the notion of a "history of salvation," tradition could be seen as unfolding the divine Word in an unbroken rectilinear process which reaches the present and carries the church on into the future.

The discovery that tradition in the Bible is diverse, with the history-of-salvation stream standing alongside a royal-covenant stream and a sapiential stream (to name but two important examples), does complicate the problem of tradition's role in mediating the meaning of Scripture. Tradition's mediation will occur in a special way which must be explained in a manner sensitive to the specific characteristics of the biblical writings, and those characteristics include what we have just described as a rich diversity of streams of tradition.

In exploring more promising ways of understanding how the dynamic meaning of Scripture reaches us through a long history of tradition, it seems best to begin concretely within the biblical writings themselves. Therefore chapters 2, 3, and 4 will examine specific examples of diverse streams of tradition in the Old Testament. From within the Bible—though not without utilizing modern methods and concepts—we shall seek to understand the significance of this diversity. Key to our understanding will be recognition of the theological significance of polarity. We shall come to see that even in the Bible, tradition is received by the community of faith not as a homogeneous system of thought, but as a tension-filled stream characterized by divergent perspectives. The significance of this tension can hardly be overestimated. For such a tradition—or what we prefer to call confessional heritage—places the life of the community within a lively field of tension between diverse perspectives. Sensitive to the importance of each of the streams of the past, and at the same time aware of God's abiding presence, the community seeks to blaze a path into the future as an expression of its desire to be faithful to the covenant with the living God. Above all, this effects a state of openness to the new activities of God. The past does not furnish a simple blueprint, but it sketches a model for a communal life of faithful response to the new in light of the old. From the past are derived paradigms of faithful responses in earlier periods and an overall pattern of divine purpose which locates the new generation in an age-long trajectory of divine activity. But the newness of the contemporary moment of communion with the living God is safeguarded by the form in which the confessional heritage reaches the present, the form of diversity and polarity constituting a field of tension where the life of faith is not possession but openness and dedication to a fitting faithful response. In chapters 5, 6, and 7 and in the appendix, I shall illustrate how the contemporary community of faith can live within the eschatological field of tension which it inherits from its confessional heritage.

For the believer who does not take offense at the initial appearance of heightened complexity, this view of heritage or tradition can foster a proper hermeneutical posture. This we can see by once again returning to the three insights derived from modern hermeneutical study. If the dynamic, richly diverse stream of tradition which reaches us from our biblical heritage fosters in us an attitude of openness to God's ongoing activity, then the other two closely related insights of general hermeneutics find their proper application: The subjective dimension of the monuments of our confessional heritage call into question individual prejudices, parochial public interests, and unjust institutional structures. And the power of language to call forth a world more in harmony with ultimate reality finds hearers vulnerable and open to the address of divine Word.

In the final analysis, I believe that thoughtful believers will be receptive to an understanding of the meaning of Scripture which incorporates rather than obscures the rich diversity found at the heart of the Bible itself. For such believers do not regard reality (and certainly not the Author of all reality) as a simple object to be interrogated and described. Reality, on its most basic level, is ineffable, and descriptions must strive for honesty through statements that correct each other. While our responses, and those of our ancestors in the faith, are diverse, we nevertheless affirm the oneness of God and the unity of God's purpose for creation. Believing that God has been active in a purposeful way over the span of history leads us to the fascinating study of the traditions responding in their special ways to that activity. That each tradition is imbued with the particular world view of its time and is expressive of the particular social and religious presuppositions of its sponsoring group comes as no surprise if we affirm the concrete historicality of every expression of reality. This adds urgency to understanding each tradition in its specificity and allowing the various traditions in their rich diversity to witness to the activity of the Author of all life, who as an active God surely is manifested, but who as the one true God is always clothed in majesty and mystery. Taking seriously the polarities found at the heart of Scripture is one way of allowing ourselves to be addressed by our confessional heritage concerning its interaction with God while yet safeguarding the mystery of the One who causes that interaction.

Not only do such polarities then make possible deeper insight into the rich biblical vision of God than can views which reduce the diversity through superficial harmonization; they also relate more poignantly to the multifaceted complexity which thoughtful moderns see reflected in their experiences. Properly understood, the Bible enters modern life not as a summons to retreat into an archaic world of primordial simplicity. Rather it provides the staging point for engagement at the heart of life out of dedication to the purposes of a God who breaks the bonds that drag individuals and societies to perdition, and who draws the responsive toward a life of wholeness, experienced as the all-sufficiency of divine grace and expressed as self-transcending service wherever human need is encountered.

CHAPTER 2

Kings and Prophets
in Tension, and the
Development of the
Form/Reform Polarity

A MODERN DILEMMA: CONFLICTING UNDERSTANDINGS OF SCRIPTURE

A battle is about to begin. The lines are being formed. The issues at stake involve religious beliefs. But in this modern-day Armageddon we witness not the knights of Christendom lined up against the forces of the Antichrist but Christians pitted against Christians. It is to be a "Battle for the Bible." Harold Lindsell's book by this title popularized that phrase and clearly articulates the position of one side of the conflict. Evangelical Christianity has traditionally held to the inerrancy and infallibility of the Bible as its central defense against heresy. According to Lindsell, only strict adherence to that position will preserve evangelical Christianity from heresy in the future.[1]

One may dispute Lindsell's generalization by citing questions which Christian theologians like Luther raised concerning the authoritativeness of certain parts of Scripture. But one should not do so as a means of evading Lindsell's basic challenge. For while inerrancy is not as universally a part of the history of classical biblical interpretation as he maintains, it is nevertheless true that for the vast majority of Christians, clerical and lay, intellectual and common, from the early centuries of the church down to the eighteenth century, the Bible was interpreted literally: what the Bible said was an accurate description of what had happened, and what had happened remained binding on the church for all time. Lindsell's challenge, which deserves to be taken seriously, reads: Why should a position which has served the community of faith for so many centuries be questioned or revised by Christian biblical scholars? Is not such questioning plainly and simply a departure from true faith?

14

One way to answer these fundamental questions is to point out that biblical scholars have not invented such problems. They have arisen in the minds of thoughtful believers as a result of conflicts they perceive between biblical statements on the one hand and modern experiences and interpretations of experience on the other. But then the reply would certainly follow: whatever the source of the questioning, the church must stand up for the traditional position, for it represents the unchanging truth. Such a reply focuses the question on a fundamental point: any departure from a traditional position must be defended on the basis of principles inherent within the faith itself. Now if study of biblical traditions leads one to recognize that the entire history of our confessional heritage has been characterized by development from antecedent traditions to new formulations, it follows that change cannot be ruled out of consideration on a priori grounds. But any specific change must be demonstrated as growing out of the central dynamic of our confessional heritage before it can be commended to the community of faith.

The sad spectacle of Christians mustered to engage in battle against Christians can be replaced by the far more heartening scene of Christians gathering in the spirit of loving concern to debate important issues. What is necessary is for contestants on the one side to admit that all change urged by the *Zeitgeist* is not necessarily faithful to the confessional heritage, even as those on the other side admit that the desire to control divine revelation by imposition of human doctrines—whether these be inherited from hoary antiquity or conceived by a new outpouring of spiritual zealousness—can detract from openness to the living God.

In every ethnic setting one hears stories similar to the one which was told in the Swedish-American community within which I grew up, and which gives lighthearted expression to a trait residing in every mortal.[2] In preaching from an Old Testament text, the local pastor referred to the meaning of a Hebrew word. After the service an elderly gentleman came to the pastor, greatly excited, with a question: "Pastor Byquist, have the missionaries now even translated God's Word from the Swedish into Hebrew?"

On numerous levels, from the trivial to the demonic, mortals seek to domesticate the *mysterium tremendum,* to visualize God as a private patron speaking their language and defending their narrow, parochial concept of ultimate truth. Neither liberals nor conservatives are immune to this malady, and hence theology must be attentive to safeguards against an activity which comes so naturally to sinful humans—casting gods in their own images.

Within religious communities seeking to derive identity and direction from a scriptural heritage, it is not uncommon for the study of the Bible to be drawn into the vortex of the struggle to cut God down to human size. The history of religion has witnessed one movement after the other, born of a struggle against oppressive structures in the name of a righteous God, only to be transformed into a partner with an order as oppressive as the one opposed earlier. The Christian church is not immune to the temptation to try to control Scripture rather than be addressed by it, to place the scholarship that studies the Bible above the Bible itself rather than learning from the Bible how a community of faith lives with an openness to God's purpose.

We find ourselves situated on the horns of a dilemma. Central to our understanding of God's self-disclosure is that process by which the foundational events and experiences of our faith were recorded and preserved for future generations. But lurking in the shadow of preservation and canonization is the danger that living Word will become dead words. Such words, gathered into a book and bound, are defined as God's words *once* spoken, God's acts *once* performed, and a definitive dogmatic structure is built around them to specify exactly what these words are to signify. What occurred in the Middle Ages and in the seventeenth and eighteenth centuries is happening in many churches again today: God's Word is no longer a living force which addresses, convicts, breaks open sterile structures, and places the community's decisions before the living God. Instead it is shoved into the straitjacket of a closed orthodoxy which it is obliged to corroborate by supplying a collection of proofs.

ALTERNATIVE SOLUTIONS: FORM VERSUS REFORM

It is because of the modern theological dilemma of conflicting understandings of Scripture that many would formulate our modern problem as a matter of choosing between mutually exclusive alternatives. Alternative One: Cast your lot with the cause of *reform,* whether in the form of social change or liberation of the personal psyche. Scripture is too easily drawn into the cause of the slaveholder, the decadent rich, the sexist oppressor. The church, as vanguard of God's liberating activity, must not derive its sense of mission from a backward glance at its Bible, but from a future vision of the kingdom to come. The rallying point of the church, therefore, is the same as that of any reform movement: a universal ideal of humaneness. Alternative Two: Owing to internal disagreement over what is universally humane, and a lack of motivation to stand up courageously for absolute standards, liberal movements unwittingly demonstrate the need for the church to take its stand on *form,* a form which is eternal because it comes from God, given in the infallible, inerrant Bible. Of course, fundamentalism is not the only version of this "form" alternative. A rigid orthodoxy which claims that its confessions and dogmatic formulations are immutable and absolute belongs here too.

In the face of these conflicting alternatives it is essential to clarify the theological stream with which one identifies. Among the various streams today is one which continues to move steadily through a wide spectrum of denominations and which refuses to reduce the gospel to either of the "pure" religions of fundamentalism or of unbiblical liberalism. The source of that stream is a gospel which long ago repudiated any legalism that leads to spiritual enslavement. Relating to a living God experienced as one who forgives sinners, this stream finds in divine grace the basis to live life amid the ambiguities of human existence without the need to reduce faith to one human principle, be it scriptural inerrancy or the authority of human reason. For Christians experiencing the church as Christ's body, a body growing daily in relation to the living God who is ever active in the world to bring the dead to life and the sinner to repentance, form and reform are not mutually exclusive alternatives at all. They constitute a tension-filled polarity which defines the very field within which the Christian lives out his or her response to God's grace.

The responsible Christian will not hesitate to acknowledge the importance of *form* in life, that ordered sphere within which life can be lived productively and in harmony with others, a dependable context within which to engage in the *re*form mandated by the gospel. Only if form excludes reform is it oppressive. In turn, pure reform without form is chaos—social, political, spiritual chaos. It is fitting for the modern Christian to continue to cherish Scripture, the catholic creeds, and the historical confessions, for they are forms which order the chaos that surrounds us. But the living, dynamic movement of God, to which they are all historical responses, leads us to accept these forms as the platform from which we carry on God's mandate of *reform* as a living expression of our sense of participation in God's purposes.

FORM AND REFORM IN THE BIBLE: INDISPENSABLE SIDES OF AN ESSENTIAL POLARITY

As passions flare and antagonists seek to form their lines within the current battle for the Bible, Christians with a critically informed appreciation of Scripture do well to ground their position within the Bible itself. Within denominations where the climate of historical study and self-critique still thrives, they must demonstrate that the form/reform polarity, encouraging a response that is both courageous and sensitive, is at the heart of Scripture itself. It is helpful in this effort to draw the distinction between historical forms on the one hand and the divine initiative and dynamic on the other, a distinction which has a long history before, outside of, and beyond all efforts at theological formulation. Such efforts stand in continuity with those of the Reformers by demonstrating that responsible study of the forms of our confessional heritage and prophetic reform are not adversaries but partners in a common mission.

As a way of giving one specific illustration of the form/reform polarity in the Bible, we turn to an examination of kings and prophets in early Hebrew religion, for the kings were characteristically guardians of form even as the prophets were advocates of reform. To understand the polarity which they represent, it is necessary to survey the origins of the Yahwistic faith (that is, faith in "Yahweh," as the God of the Hebrews was most commonly named in antiquity).

Origins

Yahwistic faith arose as a protest against a widely prevailing orthodoxy of the ancient Near Eastern world. This was a mythopoeic orthodoxy, according to which social structures were eternal, being reflections of the divine realm in the world of humans. Thus, for example, slaves were slaves as a result of a primordial order, and each stratum of society in turn had its position in an immutable structure safeguarded by the watchful eye of king and royal cult. This is not to deny that some development occurred in this world view. For example, when Babylon gained hegemony over a region formerly held by Sumerians, Marduk replaced Enlil in the cosmogonic myth. And later still, when Assyria conquered Babylon, Ashur replaced Marduk. The development, however, was not teleological, but cosmic: the alteration became a part of what was viewed within the society regulated by the myth as eternal cosmic structure. The contradiction of change within eternality was not bothersome to ancient mythopoeic thought.

The Egypt of the Pharaohs of the Mosaic period was characterized by this type of static mythopoeic orthodoxy. And the birth of the Hebrew religion is closely related to the disclosure of a new type of faith to the Hebrew slaves in Egypt. But our understanding of the depth of biblical revelation is enriched by reference to a pre-Mosaic phase of this disclosure. In the Bible this phase is presented schematically in the patriarchal stories of Genesis. In a number of Mesopotamian sources we can glimpse the historical context of this period of preparation in the movement of a group of people called "Amorites" (which can be translated "westerners," referring to their place of origin). Into the mythopoeic orthodoxy where kings were kings and slaves were slaves forever the Amorites infiltrated around 2000 B.C. From bits and pieces of evidence, we can see that they adhered to a view of the divine which contrasted sharply with that of the indigenous population. This is seen, for example, in their personal names, which are sentence names crediting a patron god with a gracious gift or act (like "God has given [a child]" or "God has delivered"). It is also seen in their genealogical lists, which preserve the lines of succession of their rulers. In the case of the earlier Sumerian king lists, the succession followed the pattern of movement from one sacred cult *place* to the next, reflecting the belief that the static form of reality which centered on the sacred place was primary. The city-state with its temple was the object of divine election. In the Amorite genealogies, succession is traced instead along the family tree, indicating that a *spacial* focus has yielded to a *temporal* focus. Divine election has come to focus on a human group, like the family of Hammurabi. When these sentence names and these genealogies from the so-called era of Abraham are taken together, we recognize the seeds of a revolutionary alternative to the static mythopoeic orthodoxy: divine presence is manifested not primarily in the immutable structures of the cult but in the changing events of history. The role of religion is no longer to deny the flux of the profane world of religious significance but is to challenge the faithful to live courageously and righteously within the events of history. And in the long progression of such events is discerned a divinely guided movement from promise to fulfillment.

We are able to recognize two types of faith at this early period. One kind engenders a cult which is dedicated to the preservation of eternal form or, in modern parlance, is devoted to order and security. Within this form-engendering faith, development involves the further exploration of a static order, which development we can designate as a "cosmic vector." The other kind of faith engenders a cult in which the deity is confessed to be active, creatively and redemptively, in the movement of time. Knowledge of the ultimate and the good involves not penetration into a changeless order, but discernment of divine activity and the unfolding of human value amid the changing realities of this world; it is committed to reform. Because of the dynamic, forward-moving thrust of this kind of faith, development within it can be described in terms of a "teleological vector."[3]

Out of Egypt

When Israelite faith was born, these two faith alternatives coexisted in the consciousness of the Hebrew slaves. We could even say that biblical faith was born of father Form and mother Reform, if it is understood that the father soon alienated his offspring by his harshness. The view of the father, the static view, was ensconced by the Egypt of the Pharaohs in a classic form which had already existed for over a millennium and was to live on for nearly as long a time thereafter. But mother Reform was latently present in the minds and aspirations of the Hebrew slaves as the result of the infiltration of Amorite folk into Egypt during the Middle Bronze Age. For these ancestors of the Hebrews fostered a view according to which the so-called eternal structures of the Pharaoh were not immune to challenge. In fact, the Hebrews preserved in oral form stories according to which the patron deity of their fathers had promised one day to give them a land of their own. This suggested to them that their slavery was not as absolute as the Pharaoh had claimed.

It is against the background of this latent, teleological view that we can understand the Hebrew epic with its account of escape from Egyptian slavery and entry into Palestine. On the basis of this view the mythopoeic orthodoxy was challenged. When the Hebrews' rebellion against the "eternal" structures of the Pharaoh met with success, they inferred from their alternative world view that this escape was a manifestation of the will of the Hebrew patron God, Yahweh. Other inferences followed: the Pharaoh's institution of slavery was evil; there was no king but Yahweh; and this divine King Yahweh was not the guardian of the privileges of the powerful but a champion of the oppressed.

In sum, at the earliest period discernible to scholarship, the Hebrews challenged the prevailing notion that religious truth was timeless and deducible from primordial events which had established eternal cosmic structures and social orders. Instead, the true and the good were to be perceived in the events of this world, events interpreted as the arena within which Yahweh was unfolding a plan for his people. This perception did not exclude a deep appreciation for the role of past heritage in the teleological interpretation of history. Indeed, if space allowed a full survey of the development of biblical faith, it would become clear that such faith unfolds precisely within the dialectical interaction between confessional heritage and new events, an interaction occurring within the community of faith as a part of their relationship with the living God.

The League Period

It was in the period of the Judges that the new dynamic which gave rise to Yahwism found an appropriate institutional form. Since there was no king but Yahweh, the leader in Israel could only be one designated by Yahweh to carry out a task in a specific emergency. This was the charismatic šôpēt ("judge," or more accurately "savior"), whose responsibility it was to respond to Yahweh's spirit by mustering the tribes to do battle when any tribe was attacked. If any son of a šôpēt tried to succeed his father, as Gideon's son Abimelech did, he was rejected by the tribes, who acted on the principle that in Israel there was to be no king but Yahweh. When the crisis abated, the freedom-loving warriors returned to their inheritance to farm and raise cattle, meeting together otherwise only to celebrate their common faith at a central shrine.

The study of early biblical law illustrates how the new world view became the basis for the life of the Hebrew community. For example, each family head was given a nāḥălāh, that is, a portion of land, which was held by inalienable right. No stronger law could have been established to safeguard against a return to slavery. A system of remission of indebtedness functioned in a similar manner. And the developing ideal of community even went so far as to safeguard strangers in the land from the type of enslavement which the Hebrews had suffered in their sojourn in Egypt: "You shall not oppress a stranger; you know the heart of a stranger, for you were strangers in the land of Egypt" (Exod. 23:9).[4] The early legal codes are remarkable in the way in which they derive the laws of community from the prior experience of deliverance: "You shall not wrong a stranger or oppress him, for you were strangers in the land of Egypt. You shall not afflict any widow or orphan. If you do afflict them, and they cry out to me, I will surely hear their cry; and my wrath will burn, and I will kill you with the sword, and your wives shall become widows and your children fatherless" (Exod. 22:21-24).

The heart of the new world view was, of course, a new concept of the divine as compassionate and on the side of the downtrodden: "If you lend money to any of my people with you who is poor, you shall not be to him as a creditor, and you shall not exact interest from him. If ever you take your neighbor's garment in pledge, you shall restore it to him before the sun goes down; for that is his only covering, it is his mantle for his body; in what else shall he sleep? And if he cries to me, I will hear, for I am compassionate" (Exod. 22:25-27).

Here we see clearly the effects of the new dynamic world view; it is dedicated to preserving an ideal of freedom and human rights experienced as deriving from a gracious act of deliverance by Yahweh, an ideal safeguarding even the rights of strangers. And just as importantly, it is an ideal construed as *developing amid new experiences,* experiences interpreted as the ongoing manifestation of divine will. This can be illustrated in terms of certain differences between the eleventh-century-B.C. Book of the Covenant (which we quoted in the Exodus passages above) and the later Deuteronomic revision of this law. In Exodus, for example, only male slaves were released from their bondage in the seventh year; a female remained a slave for life, unless the master abandoned her. In Deuteronomy, by contrast, no distinction is made: males and females are both released. Similarly, in the Book of the Covenant only males are invited to celebrate the cult festivities at the central shrine, whereas in Deuteronomy males, females, servants, children, all are invited. This dynamic movement can clearly be traced back to the new world view of these released slaves.[5]

In Israel, recitation and reenactment of the forms of tradition are not allowed to establish the pattern of a timeless mythic cycle. The message of the Exodus is a contemporary message, as indicated by a passage written five hundred years after the Exodus: "The Lord our God made a covenant with *us* in Horeb. Not with our fathers did the Lord make this covenant, but with *us,* who are *all of us* here alive *this day"* (Deut. 5:2–3, emphasis added). This epic was kept alive as present reality through reenactment and narrative amplification. In the Bible, tradition grows. Passages expand and have multiple settings in life.

The period of the Judges was a time of remarkable development along the teleological vector, with lasting breakthroughs in the area of human values. However, we must not overlook the expressions of inhumaneness: the institution of slavery continued for some several millennia after the Exodus, and the ideology of holy war continued to be used for justifying slaughter. But a significant fact is not minimized: a dynamic notion of cult replaced an essentially static one. This set the development of biblical religion on a teleological trajectory which is traceable, for example, all the way to the Emancipation Proclamation of Abraham Lincoln. We must take care to remember, however, that the dynamism of the biblical religion to which we have fallen heir is not to be confused with an inexorable process of ascent to greater and greater heights. When Israel's prophets reviewed their nation's history, they saw running alongside a history of salvation, and often interwoven with it, a history of damnation. And our record has not improved. For we as twentieth-century believers must recognize in the era after the Emancipation Proclamation our miserable failure to translate humane principles into practice. We also acknowledge, alongside rare examples in church and society of obedience to the way of the cross, a fascination with ecclesiastical triumphalism and imperialistic militarism which is more objectionable than the holy war ideology of the Israelites. Belonging to a dynamic religious heritage thus does not assure the cause of humaneness; it challenges the humane precisely because the future is suspended in such a precarious balance, calling for a response that transcends human fickleness and that is drawn toward God's creative, redemptive purpose.

"Appoint for Us a King"

In a survey of the origins of Yahwistic faith, the late eleventh century gives the appearance of being a watershed, for at that time the whole dynamic development of the period of the Judges seemed to grind to a halt. The Israelites came to their last judge, Samuel, and said, "Appoint for us a king to govern us like all the nations" (1 Sam. 8:5). Scholars who hold to the Exodus tradition as theologically normative in a rectilinear sense interpret this request as a harsh attack on Yahwism. But is it? One stream of biblical tradition supports their contention. It cites Yahweh's response, "They have not rejected you [Samuel], but they have rejected me from being king over them" (1 Sam. 8:7), and from there Yahweh goes on to warn the people of the highhanded ways of kings. But another stream of biblical tradition sees the king as a deliverer from the threat of annihilation: "Now the day before Saul came, the Lord had revealed to Samuel: 'Tomorrow about this time I will send to you a man from the land of Benjamin, and you shall anoint him to be prince over my people Israel. He shall save my people from the hand of the Philistines; for I have seen the affliction of my people, because their cry has come to me' " (1 Sam. 9:15–16). Thus the Bible, in preserving this diversity, is more complex and, I think, more profound than uncritical liberationists who speak only of revolution and forget the concomitant human need for security, nurture, order, and form. Now we must examine the form/reform polarity as it unfolds in the early monarchy, for this is a necessary step toward understanding kings and prophets in the Bible.

The breakthroughs to new levels of egalitarian and humane values in the period of the Judges are very significant, but lest we devote exclusive attention to the reform side of the polarity, we must recognize that they developed under unique circumstances. In the twelfth century B.C., the tribes, once established in the land, lived in freedom from the menace of the great empires. Both Egypt and the great nations of Mesopotamia were in eclipse. The tribes were able to develop their communal ideal relatively free from outside disruption. What threats arose were handled by the militia, which further strengthened their dedication to reform Yahwism.

A different actor, however, entered the stage in the mid-eleventh century B.C., ending Israel's honeymoon with an egalitarian confederacy. The new actor was actually a hydra, for the Sea Peoples comprised different groups. But they were all being driven eastward in the tidal wave set off by the fall of the Mycenaean Empire. And they were all viciously bent on conquest. The Mittanian, Hittite, and Ugaritic Empires fell, and the twentieth Egyptian dynasty shook, as the Sea Peoples swarmed over the land. Among them were the Philistines. As they pressed further and further into lands claimed by the Hebrew tribes, and as the Hebrew militia under the charismatic *šôpēt* encountered one humiliating military defeat after another, the people came to recognize the need for order and form. Here was a value, indeed, which their grim experiences with slavery had led them to distrust and to associate with the very source of oppression in the world. But now, staring into the jaws of the Philistine war machine, a machine led by kings and manned by professional soldiers, these freedom- and reform-loving former slaves could no longer live in the virginal purity of their charismatic confederacy. They needed the form of a sophisticated bureaucracy. They needed a king! The Israelites of Samuel's age felt the force of world politics driving them away from the consistent application of egalitarian ideals derived from their experience of deliverance, and casting them into the ambiguities of civil maturity. The question with which Samuel and his ilk had to struggle was this: Would all the freedoms, and all the laws which safeguarded those freedoms, now have to be sacrificed to the cause of form, order, and security? The painful tension of this period is captured exquisitely in 1 Samuel. In one scene Samuel comes up to the young hero Saul, pours the anointing oil over his head, and declares: "Has not the Lord anointed you to be prince over his people Israel? And you shall reign over the people of the Lord and you will save them from the hand of their enemies round about" (1 Sam. 10:1). But in another scene the mood is very different: Samuel is commanded by Yahweh to warn the people what it will be like living under a king:

"Now then, hearken to their voice; only, you shall solemnly warn them, and show them the ways of the king who shall reign over them."

So Samuel told all the words of the Lord to the people who were asking a king from him. He said, "These will be the ways of the king who will reign over you: he will take your sons and appoint them to his chariots and to be his horsemen, and to run before his chariots; and he will appoint for himself commanders of thousands and commanders of fifties, and some to plow his ground and to reap his harvest, and to make his implements of war and the equipment of his chariots. He will take your daughters to be perfumers and cooks and bakers. He will take the best of your fields and vineyards and olive orchards and give them to his servants. He will take the tenth of your grain and of your vineyards and give it to his officers and to his servants. He will take your menservants and maidservants, and the best of your cattle and your asses, and put them to his work. He will take the tenth of your flocks, and you shall be his slaves. And in that day you will cry out because of your king, whom you have chosen for yourselves; but the Lord will not answer you in that day.

But the people refused to listen to the voice of Samuel; and they said, "No! but we will have a king over us."

(1 Sam. 8:9–20)

Thus the biblical narrative is torn between two attitudes toward kingship, and the nation was to struggle with this tension for the rest of its years.

We may want to rush in where the final editor of the Bible did not dare to tread and resolve the tension by adjudicating which side was right. Are you for kings or prophets? Declare yourselves! But that pure course was not the one followed by the editor or by the nation. The tension had to be endured. But how? Either creatively, leading to new depths of insight into the purposes of God and the human values they implied, or nihilistically, leading to the destruction of the most exciting experiment in freedom and justice which had thus far entered the stage of human history.

This crisis called for a unique counselor, and God did not abandon the people. The challenge was not one which could be met by a confederate purist, nostalgically insisting on a return to the simple ways of tribal autonomy, nor by a royal purist, enlisting support for the recasting of the rigid forms of Egyptian fleshpots in local Palestinian clay. Instead the situation called for a godly counselor who could relate all traditional forms to the dynamic reform ideals of freedom, righteousness, and equality before God, ideals which could be maintained neither apart from form nor in the context of a system of form which forced justice to bow obsequiously before a royal throne. What did the wise counselor say in this crisis?

> And all the people said to Samuel, "Pray for your servants to the Lord your God, that we may not die; for we have added to all our sins this evil, to ask for ourselves a king." And Samuel said to the people, "Fear not; you have done all this evil, yet do not turn aside from following the Lord, but serve the Lord with all your heart; and do not turn aside after vain things which cannot profit or save, for they are vain. For the Lord will not cast away his people, for his great name's sake, because it has pleased the Lord to make you a people for himself. Moreover as for me, far be it from me that I should sin against the Lord by ceasing to pray for you; and I will instruct you in the good and the right way. Only fear the Lord, and serve him faithfully with all your heart; for consider what great things he has done for you. But if you still do wickedly, you shall be swept away, both you and your king."
>
> (1 Sam. 12:19–25)

This is a remarkably subtle theological statement, filled with the tension of the form/reform polarity. Samuel's reply gives the lie to all

utopian schemes, for it is based not on nostalgic longing for the inno-
cence of the past, but on a radically historical faith. In asking for a king,
Israel acted out of a lack of trust in Yahweh. But given the sinful situation, there was no alternative to kingship. For the Hebrews had learned
that God does not act in a timeless heavenly drama, but in the stuff of
history, in the context of world affairs, in the material of sinful choices,
and within the realities of tainted structures. "Only beware, Israel,"
Samuel in effect warned. "The imperfect structures of kingship *will*
surely be the context within which Yahweh will continue to act in harmony with his redemptive purposes. But how the people live out their
response within those imperfect structures will determine whether Yahweh's acts take the form of deliverance or judgment!" Samuel goes on,
"As for me, far be it from me that I should sin against the Lord by
ceasing to pray for you; and I will instruct you in the good and the
right way" (1 Sam. 12:23).

THE BIRTH OF PROPHECY, AND CONFLICT
BETWEEN KINGS AND PROPHETS

Human sin, as that condition was intertwined with realities reaching
from the crumbling walls of Mycenae to the raging waters of the Tigris,
forced kingship upon Israel. The need for form had asserted itself. Since
the people confessed Yahweh as the one guiding the events of history,
they believed that he had acquiesced to their request for a king. But they
understood their God to have done so only with a reluctance which
warned that Israel's kingship would have to be different from that found
in Egypt or Mesopotamia; it would have to be a kingship where the
form of the king was wedded to the reform of the prophet.

It is thus no accident that in Israel prophecy was born with the emergence of kingship and died with its demise. Nor is it accidental that the
prophecy which we see in Israel is unparalleled in the rest of the ancient
Near East of the pre-Christian era.[6]

Samuel, as wise counselor, continued to guide Israel even after the
people dismissed him from office as šôpēt. He ushered Israel into this
new era by splitting his old office in two. He gave the people a king, but
the king would possess only one half of the šôpēt's function, that of a
civil ruler. Why? Because of a central theological tenet in biblical faith:
no hereditary office could possess the other half, that of being the living
channel of divine will. Only the charisma of Yahweh could designate

the bearer of that office. That is to say, there is an aspect of spirituality which cannot be poured into permanent forms, cannot be institution- alized. This is the theological basis of the birth of prophecy as the office which would keep reform alive in Israel.

According to the Samuel compromise, then, the office of *šôpēt* was divided into the two offices of prince and prophet. The first incumbent in the royal office, Saul, experienced severe difficulties. He was neither *šôpēt* (judge) nor prince nor prophet but a mixture possessing traits of all three. He came to office like a *šôpēt,* called by a prophet to deliver the tribes from an invader, but he was designated a prince. Yet he insisted on performing the religious functions of prophet and priest. Confused by the tensions and complexities of his office and nation, and unable to adapt to the delicately weighted system of checks and balances introduced by Samuel, he went mad.

David was of a different mettle. He learned well the lessons of Samuel. Samuel had made it clear that the king of Israel was to act not as an absolute monarch but as guardian over the egalitarian rights of the old tribal confederacy. To assure this function, the prophet was placed alongside the king with the kinds of powers which have always caused kings to tremble: the powers to (1) designate and depose kings, (2) declare war, and (3) hold kings accountable to the laws of the community and the ideals which those laws safeguarded.

David was skilled in dealing with the balance. He moved the sacred symbol of the confederacy into his tent sanctuary in Jerusalem, thus demonstrating continuity between the old and the new. He acquiesced to Nathan's oracle forbidding his building a temple. He retained both priestly houses of the tribal period. He repented of his sins in the sordid matter of Uriah the Hittite. But throughout his reign the struggle was intense, and the form/reform polarity threatened to come apart in more than one crisis.

A major source of conflict was the coalition of northern tribes, which never felt comfortable with kingship. In one case full rebellion broke out under Sheba's seditious cry:

> We have no portion in David,
> and we have no inheritance in the son of Jesse;
> every man to his tents, O Israel!
>
> (2 Sam. 20:1b)

For these freedom-loving northerners, David's establishment of a professional army which took their sons, his policy of taxation, and his central building programs threatened their old confederate ideals. And they had a right to fear. What made matters worse, in later life David was learning no longer from Samuel but from the Phoenicians, those kings well tutored in the absolute monarchy of the Pharaohs. The texts suggest that David began to replace the title "prince" (*nāgîd*) with the title "king" (*melek*). And increasingly he acted like a *melek,* robbing Uriah of both his precious "lamb" and his life, tightening his own control on the finances through an expanded bureaucracy run from his independent royal city of Jerusalem, enriching his coffers through ambitious campaigns of conquest and taxation, and, in a final effort to dissolve the resistance of the old tribes, instituting a census to obliterate the old tribal boundaries in favor of a more rational division into tax districts. And throughout his reign, the prophets Nathan and Gad continued to fight for the rights of the common people. They blocked David's plan to build a temple, they chastised him in the Bathsheba affair, and they foiled his plan to redistrict. By the time of David's death, the outcome of the threatening bifurcation of form and reform was by no means certain. If anything, the signs augured ill, for the transition to Solomon was achieved by court intrigue, blood, and the sword.

The sword prevailed. Solomon became king. He set out immediately to dissolve the Samuel compromise in favor of form. He cut off one of the old priestly houses, the Mushite house of Abiathar, because it dared to criticize him, and he wedded crown to sacerdotal miter by retaining only the priestly house which had sworn him allegiance, the Zadokites. He obliterated the tribal boundaries by carrying out the census and redistricting which David had abandoned at the prophet Gad's behest; he constructed an elaborate court system, used Egyptian models of administration, built a Canaanite-type temple as a royal chapel, arranged countless royal marriages, and brought into the cult the foreign idols of his many wives. He even forced free Israelites into his professional army and into a corvée. In a word, he reigned like an absolute monarch in the grand style of the ancient Near East. And we get an insight into how he could get away with this when we observe that in the course of his reign we hear no word from or about the prophets. Along with the priest who begged to differ, the prophets were forced into silence. The polarity between form and reform had dissolved in favor of absolute form. A monolithic system prevailed.

Here we must take care not to overlook the benefits which accrue to a state devoted exclusively to form. Indeed, the biblical narrative did not overlook them. Israel moved back in the direction of the model of the Pharaohs, and the fleshpots of Egypt were thus made indigenous. The new privileged class ate well and enjoyed the other amenities of a tightly centralized absolute state: splendid buildings, good music, and the courtly delights of fables and proverbs. A true flowering of culture! As memories of Babylon, Rome, and Vienna corroborate, such a state can do much to titillate the finer tastes of the privileged.

From the point of view of the history of our heritage, we should also not overlook the accomplishments fostered by the Davidic house. In actual fact they are things we easily do overlook, for they develop the dimension for which we lack sensitivity, the cosmic vector with its exploration of those aspects of reality little given to change. But here we should recall the ruminations on the world of nature and on the behavior of different types of humans found in the sapiential tradition, and the penetrating insight into the heart lifted in praise of God found in the Psalms. For these we are indebted to the efforts of Solomon to maintain form, order, and prosperity.

Given such accomplishments, why did monolithic regal form collapse into ruins at Solomon's death? Because it was form purchased at a price which slaves who had experienced liberation from bondage were unwilling to pay, or again, because Solomon tried to return to a static form insulated against the leaven of prophetic reform. The dissolving of the form/reform polarity brought prosperity, but only for a rigidly stratified society controlled by the elite. It is no accident that the religious literature of the time witnessed a recrudescence of mythic themes. The static world view of myth was more appropriate to the monolithic system of absolute monarchy than the dynamic world view of the early Hebrew epic. As Israelites saw their ancient inalienable rights threatened, as they saw huge revenues from taxation poured into armies and palaces, they expressed the conviction that all the amenities of the world were of no worth if the heart of the people was lost, and that heart embraced as an irreducible value the free individual in an egalitarian community enjoying the blessings and responsibilities of the covenant relationship with God. As the first Israelites began to fall back into slavery because of inability to pay their taxes, the message was etched clearly in the minds of the people: slavery of a few will eventually lead to the reenslavement of all.

A groundswell of opposition gathered force against Solomon's son and successor, Rehoboam. Hearkening to the concern of the people, the elders traveled to Shechem to consult with Rehoboam on his coronation day. "Your father made our yoke heavy. Now therefore lighten the hard service of your father and his heavy yoke upon us, and we will serve you" (1 Kings 12:4). Here was a sincere attempt to reestablish the balance between form and reform inaugurated earlier by the Samuel compromise. Rehoboam consulted two groups for advice. The older counselors, recalling the model of limited kingship, advised, "If you will be a servant to this people today and serve them, and speak good words to them when you answer them, then they will be your servants forever" (v. 7). But the young, rash counselors gave Rehoboam the word he was seeking: "Thus shall you speak to this people who said to you, 'Your father made our yoke heavy, but do you lighten it for us'; thus shall you say to them, "My little finger is thicker than my father's loins. And now, whereas my father laid upon you a heavy yoke, I will add to your yoke. My father chastised you with whips, but I will chastise you with scorpions' " (vv. 10–11).

This placed the house of David solidly on the side of form. Indeed, the advice of the young counselors bristles with the rhetoric favored by the high priests of absolute form in every era as they admonish those daring to dissent. Thus a dynasty which replaced charismatic leadership with a royal succession was established that was to last half a millennium. A political climate ensued within which the cause of reform and egalitarian rights had a far harder time than even Samuel had feared. By the time of Uzziah, a highly stratified society had developed, in which the "studs" and "cows of Bashan" accumulated riches by trampling upon the rights of the poor and the powerless. From the temple, hymns were sung that borrowed deeply from Canaanite myth, thereby shoring up the static world view which helped preserve the eternal form of the dynasty. From the court, proverbs were recited which penetrated the wonders of the cosmos, and thus contributed to a growing body of knowledge. From temple and court, then, great advances were made in exploration along the cosmic vector. But teleological advances in the areas of freedom, justice, and reform came only from the courageous battle carried out on the fringes of the ordered society by such prophetic gadflies as Amos and Hosea. Though the ideal situation in which peace, form, and knowledge would be wedded with freedom, justice, and equality was thus lacking, the form/reform polarity was at least kept alive through the struggle which the prophets maintained against the abuses of monarchy.[7] In the course of this struggle, the concept of a righteous order expanded into a broadened vision as prophets related the rise and fall of powerful world empires to Yahweh's creative and redemptive purposes. In the faith of the people, Yahweh developed from a petty national patron to a universal God whose purposes went far beyond the mountains of Judea. In a word, there occurred the dynamic unfolding of the teleological vector in the dialectic between confessional heritage and new events, a vector with an effective force that would impel the biblical community of faith to ever-new experiences with the creator-redeemer God Yahweh.

While these developments were occurring in Judah, what was happening in the north? Among the northern tribes were freedom-loving farmers who could not tolerate Rehoboam's hard law-and-order response to the modest plea of the elders. And so they raised an old cry which had already tingled the ears of David:

> What portion have we in David?
> We have no inheritance in the son of Jesse.
> To your tents, O Israel!
> Look now to your own house, David.
> (1 Kings 12:16)

The northern tribes accordingly reinstituted the Samuel compromise. A prophet anointed one of the rebels, Jeroboam, as king. The reform party won. One might logically conclude that the biblical heritage which we have been tracing was subsequently transmitted by the northern kingdom. But this was far from the case. The north knew only the sword. One violent coup followed the other. Chaos prevailed. Order was restored only for a short time by a despotic ruler, Omri, and his dynastic successors, when they suspended the Samuel compromise! But even in the north the prophets kept up their battle as long as they could. Next to the Bathsheba affair, the most moving example of the courageous prophetic defense of the old tribal rights occurs during the reign of Ahab. The story is familiar: Ahab was coaxed by his Phoenician wife to act like a king and kill Naboth when the latter dared claim that as a free Israelite he could allow no one to take his inheritance, not even a king. Elijah could not save Naboth's life, but he did promise Ahab that his violent act would be answered in blood, for a king stood under the law of God like any other mortal.

And so it happened. The dynasty of Ahab ended in a bath of blood as the result of a coup led by a charismatic ruler named Jehu, who was designated and anointed by the prophet Elisha. But later reflection by the prophets on this bloody coup gives an intriguing insight into the nuanced interpretation of the form/reform polarity among the prophets. A half-century later the prophet Hosea reflected on this incident and condemned the zealous Jehu for his excess by announcing Yahweh's word: "I will punish the house of Jehu for the blood of Jezreel, and I will put an end to the kingdom of the house of Israel" (Hos. 1:4).

The prophets did not favor violent reform which led to chaos. They looked rather for a wedding of order *and* righteousness, the marriage of form *and* reform which would inaugurate a kingdom of shalom. They kept scanning the horizon for harbingers of such a kingdom, and at times, in Hezekiah, Josiah, and the suffering servant of Deutero-Isaiah, they felt they had come close to the Day of Yahweh. Along the tedious, disappointing path of history, however, many grew impatient and resolved the tension by opting for either pure form or pure reform. As we shall see in the next chapter, this happened especially after the destruction of the temple in 587, when the polarity began to split open. A priestly party developed a hard ideological pragmatism and drew on Persian support as it sought to crush all opposition and reestablish pre-exilic forms which safeguarded the privileged status of the Zadokite priests. Another party denounced this world and took flight in the utopian reform visions of apocalypticism. But some faithful few kept straining to keep alive the ideal of a kingdom of order *and* righteousness within the day-to-day realities of their historical community. And, thank God, some faithful few continue straining in the cause of that kingdom even today.

THE PERENNIAL STRUGGLE TO MAINTAIN
THE FORM/REFORM POLARITY

Several millenniums after the period of kings and prophets in Israel, the protagonists of both pure form and pure reform are still with us. In their own ways, they seek to conform God to their own images and to the underlying ideologies of these images. The line of the former is still the familiar one: "God's form is clear; it is laid down definitively in our interpretation of Scripture; it defines everything forever, from family structure to ecclesial structure, from geology to theology. Ask no more questions. Submit to our final formulation of divine truth, and be saved." It is not just the fundamentalists and the rigidly orthodox who preach this law. Many new movements and sects, some drawing on indigenous sources and others "turning east" for their leadership and inspiration, are conveying their versions of final authority and truth-beyond-questioning. Constant self-critique is incumbent upon every religious group to assure that form and authority are not being purchased at the price of human freedom and dignity.

The pure reform line is also familiar: "All is in decay, and the cause is the *form* of existing institutions; destroy the oppressive forms of church and society, and a blessed family of peace and goodwill will grow up like a crocus." Variations on this same reform theme are found among beatniks, peaceniks, ecoloniks, and many other dreamers who cannot tolerate ambiguity. They would have us cast all form to the wind in the hope that the naked *humanum* will rise up in a spontaneous blossoming of peace and shared prosperity.

Through the long, dark years dominated by apocalypticists and theocrats, a faithful remnant continued to hold together form and reform as interdependent aspects of a God-intended human order. They discerned that the theology of the formalists was shallow, as if God's mystery could be weighed in a tin cup, and that the anthropology of the pure reformers was naive, as if humanity were essentially sinless, innocent, and inhibited only by the existence of ecclesial structures and social forms.

In the period between 500 B.C. and A.D. 20 it was the faithful remnant which maintained the form/reform polarity and thus engendered an eschatological openness which was able to recognize a wonderfully strange new act of God. The faithful remnant beheld a Messiah who came not in the *usual* form of a dazzling king, but as a unique kind of humble and suffering king, not as a fiery prophet destroying all forms of the past, but as a king-prophet recognizing the abiding value of Torah and even the place of Caesar. As we shall see in chapter 4, in Christ form and reform were held in creative tension, as form preserved a context for reform, and reform safeguarded against form's being perverted into an instrument of oppression. This is the basis of those tensions in the Gospels between Torah and history, realized eschatology and futuristic eschatology, Son of God and Son of man. In a profound and perfectly fitting way, this tension has been preserved in the christological formula "true God, true man."

As heirs of this heritage we are called to be a special kind of presence in this world, not a defensive community bent on asserting our superiority by proclaiming an ideology of pure form or a utopia of pure reform. Our identity has sufficient grounding in grace to live within the tension which alone is true to the life of faith, one that treasures the sacred forms of the past but refuses to put them in the place of the one true God who is attentive to "the least of these my brethren."

As heirs of this heritage we are not intimidated by those who in the name of the reformed, godless *humanum* would ridicule our devotion to an ancient heritage. Our hearts can burn with a compassion for the needy equal to theirs without our casting to the wind our rich forms for their slick slogans. Nor are we intimidated by the peddlers of a square form of arrogant legalism when they judge us as unevangelical because we dismiss their doctrine of inerrancy as a product of bad biblical theology. The Word upon which our salvation is founded is dependable, not because we have contained it in a dogmatic box, but because it is a living Word which is self-authenticating in the mysterious manner of everything that proceeds from the one true God.

In this community we conduct neither witch hunts nor king hunts nor prophet hunts. We recognize the contributions of the modern counterparts of both kings and prophets, and realize that even witches sometimes speak wisely. We accept the role of those who attend to the preservation and interpretation of our ancient forms and symbols, even as we acknowledge the importance of guardians of social and political forms. But at the same time we lend an open ear to prophetic types who subject our forms to the critique of social justice, world peace, and divine righteousness; and we are not abrupt in dismissing the voice of the one who calls us to repent, knowing that the true prophet is often not recognized until he or she tells a simple tale of the slaughter of an innocent lamb and then with penetrating eyes informs us, "You are the one!" Nor do we belittle the longings of those myriad folk around us who, far from being kings or prophets, are tugged by a sense of justice but at the same time want to live securely, want to side with the oppressed here and abroad, and at the same time want their children to inherit a prosperous, ordered society. We seek instead to nurture their sensitivity to the compatibility of form and reform, of stability and justice. As Jezreel, Athens, Rome, Dachau, and Belfast teach us, it is people in the home, the shop, and the university who determine what type of climate will exist in the church and in the land, whether it be one of reason which will invite kings and prophets to interact creatively, one of a stubborn drive for order and privilege which will invite the final solutions of the demagogue, or one of violent zeal which will destroy oppressive structures only to create a chaos conducive to even greater oppression.

The form/reform polarity is not a magic wand that will solve all theological and social problems. Indeed, it will complicate problems for which our world offers numerous "simple" solutions. But the resulting complexity will place us in a posture fitting for those called to be Christ's body in a suffering world. It is a posture that will assure openness both to God's Word revealed through the sacred forms of our ancient heritage and to Christ's advent in the sighs of the hungry child and the broken in spirit. It will be a posture that will keep us open to our dependence on each other in the sensitive task of discerning a fitting response to God's current activity in our world. It is a posture in which we as a Christian community will neither reign as proud kings nor destroy as fiery prophets, but will seek rather to be the embodiment in the world of the Prophet/King who found obedience in reeducating the empowered and in raising up the lowly and the rejected. If we rest our lives solely upon God's grace, we will eschew the type of obedience which is but a proclamation of false pride. Rather we will obey with the steady courage that bears the weight of the faltering with quiet understanding. We will follow our vision of God's kingdom while relating readily to the day-to-day concerns of our neighbors. Grounded in the sacred forms of our heritage and trusting in God's cosmic order, we will welcome growth and reform as a challenging aspect of being children of the living God, drawn toward a kingdom in which peace finally will be wedded with righteousness.

CHAPTER 3

Apocalyptic Seers and
Priests in Conflict,
and the Development of
the Visionary/Pragmatic
Polarity

THE PROPHETIC TRANSFORMATION OF A
STATIC NOTION OF FORM INTO
AN ESCHATOLOGICAL VISION

Hebrew faith in Yahweh found its earliest expression in a movement which challenged the mythopoeic orthodoxy of the Pharaohs with a new confession: Yahweh is a God who champions the cause of the oppressed and who has created a people from naught. In this way a world dominated by form was invaded by a powerful teleological reform impulse.

Later crises became the occasion for the pendulum to swing back in the direction of form, now under the aegis of indigenous Hebrew kings. The reform impulse at the heart of early Yahwism was kept alive only through the courageous efforts of the prophets who dared oppose all pure forms of royal ideology.

We noticed from the example of Hosea, however, that the "written" prophets did not overlook the necessity for the preservation of appropriate forms to assure a suitable context for their *reform* efforts. As the pentecostal depends on the element of stability contributed by the Anglican, or the flower child depends on the monthly allowance from his hardworking parents, the prophets carried on their important reform activity within the stability assured by the monarchy. Therefore Hosea could look back to the Jehu revolution and condemn it as a case of prophetic reform zeal transgressing the limits of sobriety.

From Hosea's careful balancing of the polarity it is only a step to Isaiah of Jerusalem. Isaiah was trained in the ways of the royal court;

he rubbed shoulders with kings and princes. He advised them in matters of state. But while assuming form as a God-given dimension of personal and communal life, his entire energy was devoted to reforming *sinful* structures on the basis of the classical Yahwistic ideals deriving from the League.

While prophets like Hosea recognized the need for an element of structure or form, the teleological thrust inherent in their Yahwistic heritage made it very difficult for them simply to adopt the concept of form held by kings. For this ultimately would undermine their dedication to the ongoing reform mandated by the covenant God Yahweh. After all, form for ancient Mesopotamian and Egyptian kings was derived from a normative primordial event preserved in the timeless myth. Even Judean kings derived their concept of form from a notion of dynasty predicated on an eternal covenant established by God at the beginning of the Davidic monarchy. Frequently this notion in turn was buttressed by an appeal to archaic mythic themes.

As Yahwists who recognized the need for some degree of structure and form in the community even while harboring a deep suspicion of notions tying form to definitive events of the past, the prophets became the agents of an extremely important development in biblical faith: the *eschatologization* of the notion of form. Life indeed required a bonding and cohesiveness which was capable of warding off the unrelenting threats of chaos. But locating the source of that bonding in a definitive past event predicated life on a static norm which halted all spiritual development. Such a static, backward-looking posture contradicted the dynamic reform element derived from Israel's central experience—God acting in history to break oppressive structures and to create new forms of society and individual life. Henceforth, the prophets were to look not to an immutable form from the past for their models and patterns, but to a vision of a gracious God working out plans for creation within the divine council, and effecting those plans through intense engagement with Israel within the context of the covenant relationship.

The history of the eschatologization of form is a long one. Its roots lie in the early conflicts between the protagonists of a pure form of monarchy and defenders of the egalitarian values of the League. Under the tutelage of Samuel, the eschatologization of form came to be embodied in a uniquely Israelite ideal of kingship which bound the stabilizing qualities of kingship to the cherished values of former slaves. This lofty ideal of kingship seemed destined to collide with the realities of kingship, and so it did. With few exceptions, it was diluted, contradicted, and even spurned by kings of both the north and the south. Nevertheless, in the hopes of fervent Yahwists, the ideal of a righteous king did not die; neither was it compromised to fit existing realities. It was rather elaborated and refined as the faithful turned to the counsel of God for assurance that the reign of a peace that was wedded with righteousness, as adumbrated in their early experiences and inferred from their notion of covenant, would one day be established by a faithful anointed one (that is, messiah).

Thus it was that the common practice of recourse to a cosmogonic myth for a concept of order and form was replaced by the dynamic eschatological vision of the prophets. This is not to imply that the tension between the two sides of the form/reform polarity would be eliminated by the eschatologization of the form element, for even a vision of the future can be clothed in static categories by accommodating to the mythologoumenon *Endzeit wird Urzeit* (the eschaton will be a return to the primordial). Whenever followers of a seer were invited to abandon their involvement in this world and escape into a vision of the heavenly realm, that mythologoumenon was reemerging. Eschatologization of the form element could avoid *remythologization* only if a lesson of early Yahwism was remembered: Yahweh takes the events of this world very seriously, and hence the vision of God's ideal kingdom urged translation into the realities of everyday life. But translation within the covenant relationship could leave neither earthly structures nor heavenly vision unaffected, as the history of prophecy indicates. As *form* was transformed by *reform* in Israel's earlier history, in the era of late prophecy *vision* was subjected to *revision* in the process of prophetic translation. God's people would continue to be drawn forward by a vision of the Kingdom of God, but the interpretation of contemporary events as stages on the way toward that kingdom led in turn to an ongoing revision of the eschatological hope.

Thus the community faithful to God came to realize that it could avert the threat of chaos by conforming to a form of existence toward which God was drawing his creation. In this future vision the past was not forgotten, for it was the belief of the prophets that Yahweh, in his future acts, would be faithful to his earlier acts and promises. Past and future, like form and reform, were not irreconcilable but stood in lively tension with one another.

The significance of the future-orientation of prophetism can hardly be overemphasized. It assured that the form dimension of life, which provided an essential bonding and social cohesiveness, would no longer be derived from a static, primordial reality conducive to spiritual inertia and social stagnation. Even those divinely ordained foundational structures which provided life with a dependable context were being drawn into more adequate forms and configurations. For the faithful of Israel, this dynamic ontology did not raise the specter of chaos. To be sure, change on such a fundamental level would have been tantamount to chaos for a devotee of a mythopoeic cult. But such a threat was not experienced by the Yahwists, for they derived from their confessional heritage the conviction that the one transforming life was the designer of a dependable plan. Change was the sign not of disintegration of life's foundations but of God's purposeful activity, whether in deliverance of the oppressed, in judgment of the unrepentant, or in the commissioning of new servants of divine will. Reality, though underway, was nevertheless ultimately dependable. Events which appeared to be evidence to the contrary were thus studied as instructive of a deeper insight into the often mysterious purposes of a God who could audaciously announce to an exiled and defeated people,

> . . . My counsel shall stand,
> and I will accomplish all my purpose.
> (Isa. 46:10b)

DIVINE WORD AND WORLD:
THE PROPHETIC IMPETUS FOR A
VISIONARY/PRAGMATIC POLARITY

As the royal protagonists of form were reminded of the historical orientation of Yahwism by the reform activities of the prophets, so too those who received a vision of the new forms of reality toward which God was drawing his people found in their heritage an impetus to draw connections between that vision and the world of historical events. That is to say, the prophets felt obliged to relate their vision to the pragmatic realities of society and world. The vision was not taken to be an invitation to escape involvement in the world, but furnished a program for responsible activity within the political, social, and religious structures of life. Thus it is that prophets instruct us in a second polarity at the heart of Scripture, what we have above called a vision/revision polarity, but which in light of the translation of the vision expected of the prophet also can be called a visionary/pragmatic polarity.

As we now turn to examine this second polarity more closely, we detect a tendency in ancient Israel, which persists down to our own day, to split the polarity (even as the form/reform polarity has often been split) into its component, "pure" aspects. Especially at times of crisis and in the face of developments that threaten to break continuity with orders of the past, there is a common tendency for factions within a religious community to dissolve the polarity. Instead of simultaneously embracing a vision of an ideal order intended by God and working diligently within the order of the mundane world, the split leads to opposing parties. Some use the vision as an avenue of escape from social responsibilities. Others reduce the vision to fit pragmatic realities and human possibilities. A study of visionary apocalypticists and reductionary pragmatists is no mere exercise in ancient historiography. Contemporary society is woefully split along similar lines, and all too few are visionary-pragmatists, capable of holding together the tension as they work for responsible change while at the same time being guided by a hope whose final grounding is in divine providence. As confused moderns look to their churches for signposts to guide them along paths found on none of the maps available in the agora, it is incumbent upon the pastors and teachers of those churches to be attentive to the trajectory and the paradigms plotted in the Bible.

THE POLARITY DISSOLVED BY APOCALYPTICISM

A logical starting point for an examination of the visionary/pragmatic polarity is a description of the posture of those who dissolve the polarity in favor of escape into the vision. The posture is that of the apocalyptic seers and their followers. The works they have left to posterity are commonly designated "apocalyptic."

The Apocalyptic Consciousness

Apocalyptic describes a form of literary expression employed by people knocked off balance by crisis in life and groping for words to explain a world which seems to totter on the edge of the abyss. It is further characterized by the fact that explanation and hope are found not within the context of historical events, but by reference beyond this world to an order above or below, the realm of heaven or the realm of the arcane.

Amos Wilder, as a soldier caught in the convulsion of the battlefield in World War I, gives expression to the apocalyptic mode in these lines:

There we marched out on haunted battle-ground,
There smelled the strife of gods, were brushed against
By higher beings, and were wrapped around
With passions not of earth, all dimly sensed.

There saw we demons fighting in the sky
And battles in aerial mirage,
The feverish Very lights proclaimed them by,
Their tramplings woke our panting, fierce barrage.

Their tide of battle, hither, thither, driven
Filled earth and sky with cataclysmic throes,
Our strife was but the mimicry of heaven's
And we the shadows of celestial foes.[1]

Engulfed in carnage which belies the most basic values held by the human heart, entangled in a world insanely reeling on the brink, explanations withheld by earthly reasoning are discerned by recourse to superterrestrial spheres: these events, alas, reflect realities of celestial conflict.

The Pragmatic Consciousness

Contrast this expression of life on the edge of the abyss to the posture of those who dissolve the tension by a strictly pragmatic ordering of life: all aspects of existence are firmly and securely in control, ordered, rational, and dependable. In Alexander Pope's *Essay on Man,* for example, the closed heroic couplet contributes to the sense of a world ordered in all its parts:

All are but parts of one stupendous whole,
Whose body nature is, and God the soul;
That, changed through all, and yet in all the same;
Great in the earth, as in th' ethereal frame,
Warms in the sun, refreshes in the breeze,
Glows in the stars, and blossoms in the trees,
Lives through all life, extends through all extent,
Spreads undivided, operates unspent;
Breathes in our soul, informs our mortal part,
As full, as perfect, in a hair as heart;
Submit.—In this, or any other sphere,

Secure to be as blest as thou canst bear;
Safe in the hand of one disposing Power,
Or in the natal, or the mortal hour.
All nature is but art, unknown to thee;
All chance, direction, which thou canst not see;
All discord, harmony not understood;
All partial evil, universal good:
And, spite of pride, in erring reason's spite,
One truth is clear, WHATEVER IS, IS RIGHT.[2]

This is a description of the ordered world of the Age of Reason. The structures of this world are sound, supportive of life, and the mind can grasp explanations within categories available to human reasoning.

The Human Life in Search of a Foundation

Many people are intrigued by these diametrically opposed perceptions of life because they represent types which people can readily identify, around and within themselves. On one side there are the pragmatic, rational people, coldly efficient, giving directions in restrained tones and channeling energies toward carefully controlled objectives. On the other there are those suffering souls clutching threads of hope which disintegrate in the very grip that desperately tries to hold them. Many today have mastered an art which the world of the successful seeks to impose on its apprentices, that of wearing the mask of control while suppressing volcanic feelings of the arcane within their hearts. They stare into a thousand mirrors, all of which reflect back not the mask of control but the frightened face of the child. Out of this quandary many are led to a great deal of confusion and fright concerning their own identity. Dietrich Bonhoeffer, as he watched from a prison cell a world driven toward destruction by madmen, gave expression to the type of confusion being experienced by many sensitive moderns today:

Who am I? They often tell me
I would step from my cell's confinement
calmly, cheerfully, firmly,
like a squire from his country house.

Who am I? They often tell me
I would talk to my warders
freely and friendly and clearly,
as though it were mine to command.

Who am I? They also tell me
I would bear the days of misfortune
equably, smilingly, proudly,
like one accustomed to win.

Am I then really that which other men tell of?
Or am I only what I know of myself?
restless and longing and sick, like a bird in a cage,
struggling for breath, as though hands were compressing my throat,
yearning for colors, for flowers, for the voices of birds,
thirsting for words of kindness, for neighbourliness,
trembling with anger at despotisms and petty humiliation,
tossing in expectation of great events,
powerlessly trembling for friends at an infinite distance,
weary and empty at praying, at thinking, at making,
faint, and ready to say farewell to it all.

Who am I? This or the other?
Am I one person today and tomorrow another?
Am I both at once? A hypocrite before others,
and before myself a contemptible woebegone weakling?
Or is something within me still like a beaten army,
fleeing in disorder from victory already achieved?

Who am I? They mock me, these lonely questions of mine.
Whoever I am, thou knowest, O God, I am thine.[3]

In these words comes to expression the courage of a prophet who refuses to let the most adverse of human experiences seduce him into espousing the tension-free religions of the pure pragmatist or the pure visionary. The reason he can live within such a tension-filled polarity is revealed in the final line: his identity and need for security are not satisfied by flight into the escapist's vision or by the pragmatist's accommodation, but are grounded solely in his knowledge of belonging to God. Upon this foundation he finds a life which is both faithful to God and authentically human.

The probing question "Who am I?" thus opens up the universal question of what it is to be human. Is the paragon of humanity the power broker, who exercises perfect control while ordering objects around in perfect harmony with nature's forces? Or is it the suffering soul pouring out apocalyptic strophes from a sea of untamed crosswinds that sweep life toward dark and uncharted waters?

The former option, that of the efficiency expert in perfect control, is much in vogue these days. But can it cope with life when the harmony snaps, when lives are acted upon by forces beyond our control, when people are engulfed by personal or communal tragedy? Hardly. Indeed, those who have insulated their consciousness against suffering and lack the capacity to empathize with victims of tragedy are often the ones least equipped to respond to hardship. It is widely acknowledged that many who have suffered most profoundly and, having been driven by tragedy to reflect on the hidden dimensions of life, discover an abiding source of hope and strength are often the most trustworthy guides for others experiencing tragedy. People continue to turn to the writings of Bonhoeffer not because they find brilliant optimism, but because they recognize a courage to *be* even when the last optimist succumbs to self-doubt. There they find hope even when events prod them to come to the same conclusion Bonhoeffer himself was driven to shortly before being subjected to the Nazis' final solution: "There cannot be anyone who has not either in his work or in his private life had some sort of experience of the increasingly impatient attacks of the forces of the Antichrist."[4]

At a time when purveyors of various success formulas compete with prophets of doom for an audience, increasing numbers are being drawn to apocalyptic literature because it refuses to cover over the shadow sides of life with bright frescoes portraying idyllic harmony. It dares to address the tempest, to describe its face, and even to trace its path back to its primordial haunts.

Nor is the thoughtful response to the apocalyptic mode unmitigated enthusiasm. Apocalyptic visions led throngs of unarmed innocent children into the sharp steel swords of Muslim armies. Apocalyptic dreams played a role in transforming a vision of justice and freedom into decay in Jonestown. Apocalyptic books lead middle-class Americans, seeking to replace a spiritual vacuum with meaning, to utopian escapism and irresponsible abdication of social responsibilities. Those who use the apocalyptic mode in attempting to address the tempest arrest our attention but also our suspicion. How can one distinguish between the authentically human dimension and the seeds of cowardly escapism in apocalyptic? This question can be addressed adequately only on the basis of the biblical roots of the problem, for it arises out of the visionary/pragmatic polarity and the transformation of prophecy into apocalyptic in Israel.

The Biblical Roots of Apocalyptic

The first thing discovered in a careful study of biblical evidence is that the Bible offers no facile answer. For the view of life which unfolds through the latter epochs of biblical history, as through the earlier, is not a simple phenomenon which can be reduced to a single proposition. The richness of the biblical witness here, as in the case of conflicts between kings and prophets, can be preserved only by recognizing a field of tension as the context within which the faithful and authentically human life can be lived. Faithfulness and authenticity, in biblical understanding, implied awareness of an ideal order of reality against which all mundane structures were to be measured and evaluated. But being a faithful and full human in the biblical sense also involved persistence in seeking to translate one's vision of that order into the day-to-day realities of this world. Thus life was lived within the tension between a *vision* of a divine order which wedded peace with justice and a *pragmatism* which dealt seriously with social, political, and ecclesiastical structures as the stuff within which God was active to effect God's purposes.

This creative tension between the visionary and the pragmatic was not a timeless characteristic of all ancient Near Eastern religions, something that Israel merely inherited. We have already noted that there was a marked tendency among the cults of Israel's neighbors, the Egyptians, Hittites, Babylonians, and Canaanites, to depreciate the mundane and prefer the timeless realm of the gods. The cult in those cultures focused attention away from the changing, temporal events of history toward the great timeless cycles preserved in myth, which repeated the primordial pattern of alternation between sterility and fertility, chaos and order, death and life. In the ritual of the cult, celebrants sought to participate in the festivities of the gods as a means of being drawn away from the flux of time into the eternality of divine space.

It was a major spiritual revolution when the early Hebrews challenged the then-universal notion that the gods exercised their power in upholding the structures of absolute monarchy. According to these slaves who had successfully challenged the Pharaohs' myth, God championed the cause of the *oppressed* through saving acts in history. The implications which flowed from this new belief were profound: religion is not subservient to the static form of absolute monarchy but is devoted to a dynamic force at work in this world to transform laws, institutions, and beliefs according to an unfolding divine plan. The seer is one who perceives this plan with uncommon clarity, but since this plan is conceptualized, not as a static form derived from a primordial event which is to be handed down in perpetuity without change, but rather as a creative and redemptive dynamic which unfolds amidst the events of history, the prophet in Israel was one who exercised the responsibility of statesman by interpreting how the divine order seen in the vision was to be translated into the structures of community and world. Therefore, in comparison with the mythopoeic cults of antiquity, one can speak in a special sense of the secularization of religion in the Bible. No longer does religion call people out of the profane into the sacred space of the temple as its essential function; it commissions them rather to vocations right in the midst of the profane, which, because it is the arena of God's activity, is a holy realm.

As a clear example of the prophetic perspective that binds in creative tension a vision of an unfolding ideal order and a sense of commitment to the pragmatic realities of this world, one can take the case of the eighth-century prophet Isaiah. When called to be a prophet of Yahweh, Isaiah had a visionary experience which placed him in the presence of the council of the divine beings as they deliberated on their plans. This was the ancient way of picturing the divine realm, as an assembly of divine beings which convened to discuss and act on problems relating to the order of the universe. In Israel, Yahweh alone was considered a god, the other council members having been assigned the subservient roles of angelic advisors and messengers. Thus in chapter six we see Isaiah envisioning the ideal realm from which this world receives its direction and meaning: "I saw the Lord sitting upon a throne, high and lifted up" (v. 1). The prophet's reaction is one of dread and a sense of awful unworthiness, but he is purfiied and then hears Yahweh address the assembly: "Whom shall I send, and who will go for us?" (v. 8). Isaiah volunteers, and we recognize vividly that in the Bible human messengers are drawn into the purposes of the Deity as those who translate divine plans into historical events and human experiences. "Here am I! Send me" is Isaiah's response, whereupon Yahweh gives the prophet his instructions: "Go, and say to this people . . ." (vv. 8–9).

According to this biblical view of reality, an essential aspect of religious experience is a vision of God's purpose, for decisions made solely on the basis of human factors, like revenues, armies, and coalitions, lead to internal corruption and vulnerability to foreign aggressors.

To those acting solely upon pragmatic considerations Isaiah delivered these words:

> Woe to the rebellious children . . .
>   who carry out a plan, but not mine;
> and who make a league, but not of my spirit, . . .
> to take refuge in the protection of Pharaoh,
>   and to seek shelter in the shadow of Egypt!
>   (Isa. 30:1–2)

> Woe to those . . .
> who trust in chariots because they are many
>   and in horsemen because they are very strong,
> but do not look to the Holy One of Israel
>   or consult the Lord!
>   (Isa. 31:1)

> In returning and rest you shall be saved;
> in quietness and in trust shall be your strength.
>   (Isa. 30:15)

The policy of the faithful is grounded, therefore, in a vision of God's governance of the world, in a sense of history's movement toward peace wedded with justice under the providence of the Lord of all.

But note as well that the lofty vision does not in itself delineate the realm within which the responsible life is to be lived. The vision is but a staging point where the prophet is equipped for the true human vocation, which is in the world of real events. The prophet is not allowed to linger in the temple, to bask in the splendor of the visionary experience. For the vision is no sooner received than the command goes forth, "Go, and say to this people . . . ," and Isaiah finds himself right back in the middle of day-to-day responsibilities, counseling Ahaz, admonishing the people, and in myriad ways living as a full participant in the affairs of his community and nation.

This example from the classical prophetic period in Israel indicates that the apocalyptic vision of being drawn *from* this world order into an ideal heavenly order is *not* the perspective of the prophets. The prophetic vision delineates an ideal order, to be sure, but concludes with a commission which describes not escape from, but radical engagement *in*, the structures of this world. Possession of the vision of divine purpose, however, is not an incidental matter: it radically conditions *how* one engages in the human enterprise, whether fatalistically and apathetically

or with hope, conviction, and courage. The vision is perverted only if used as an excuse to retreat from life into the quiet rest of a timeless utopia.

The prophetic perspective with its careful balancing of visionary and pragmatic aspects does not resolve, but in fact draws attention to, another problem—verification of the truthfulness of the vision. Jeremiah and Hananiah both proclaimed words they claimed to have received from Yahweh, but the messages were diametrically opposed to each other. And the Bible cites many other instances of "false" prophets. What criteria can be used to determine truth and falsehood when one is dealing with something as elusive as a vision of divine intention? Jeremiah finally concluded that history would determine which vision had been correct. For people who are faced with making decisions vis-à-vis conflicting visions *before* history has applied its verification principle, the community of faith offers certain guidelines. One is the perspective of the ages embodied in the confessional heritage, with its trajectory of divine purpose in the past serving to guide in the discernment of divine intention in the present, and with its paradigmatic events offering helpful analogies to contemporary experiences. Another is a broad communal basis for decision making, which safeguards against the misuse of the vision to enhance the positions of some at the expense of others.

In this process of testing the visions of the prophets, a lively dialectic will occur between the individual prophetic figure and the community. The prophet, in openness to divine prompting, challenges old forms, glimpses new avenues of divine activity, and dares to proclaim the new word. The community of believers in turn relates the prophetic challenge always to a communal setting, mindful of the welfare of all members, of the need for form as well as reform, unwilling to abandon the treasures of the past though ever open to God's new chapter in history.

As long as Israel had a homeland, a nation, and the opportunity to serve Yahweh and to strive to develop a communal ideal which would preserve the rights of the widow, the orphan, the poor, and the stranger, the prophetic perspective had a chance. We say "had a chance" rather than "thrived" because keeping it alive involved much struggle. For as we indicated in the previous chapter, many in the land, led by their kings, favored a mythic view, according to which the king was to enforce a static divine structure on the land, one predicated on a social pyramid, with king at the top and a descending order of stratified classes below. The struggle between kings and prophets was basically the struggle which has reverberated through the ages between form and reform, or in other terms, law and order and social change. Both are vital to a healthy society but they must be held in balance. If form is taken as the exclusive goal, it becomes a monolithic mechanism which leads to oppression of the weak and the underprivileged. On the other hand, if form collapses entirely, reform lapses into anarchy and chaos. The struggle between kings and prophets thus manifested a universal polarity, and the prophets were able to maintain their ideal of vision translated into pragmatic reality only as long as the nation survived.

But what happens when a nation is threatened by the abyss, by the specter of annihilation, subjugation, or internal disintegration? This threat was unleashed against the northern kingdom sooner than against the southern; in 722 B.C. Samaria fell to the Assyrian armies. The northern kingdom illustrates one result of the threat of the abyss, namely, obliteration. Through assimilation to the nations, the Yahwistic prophetic perspective died among the northern states, to be remembered only by the legend of the lost tribes of Israel and by the archaizing cult of the Samaritans.

The abyss opened its awful maw to the southern kingdom in the years 597 and 587. The decline came with shocking speed, from an era of headstrong national confidence just two decades earlier to the ignominious death of the hero-king Josiah in 609, which was followed by steady disintegration culminating in decimation of the land, destruction of the temple, and deportation of much of the population by the Babylonians in 587.

The people of Israel found themselves knocked off balance, tottering on the edge of the abyss, asking what on earth all God's promises meant anyway—all those prophetic words about trust and confidence, all the attention to temple and cult.

The responses to this cultural and spiritual anomie were divided. The pure pragmatists followed the example of the northern tribes, the path of assimilation, and thus they blended into the Babylonian populace leaving no trace of their former heritage. Some followed the route of apostasy, betraying their religious heritage in favor of a more promising theological alternative, and therefore replying to Jeremiah:

As for the word which you have spoken to us in the name of the Lord, we will not listen to you. But we will do everything that we have vowed, burn incense to the queen of heaven and pour out libations to her, as we did, both we and our fathers, our kings and our princes, in the cities of Judah and in the streets of Jerusalem; for then we had plenty of food, and prospered, and saw no evil. But since we left off burning incense to the queen of heaven and pouring out libations to her, we have lacked everything and have been consumed by the sword and by famine.

(Jer. 44:16–18)

Some adopted the response of syncretism, as we see from the Jewish temple community at Elephantine in Egypt, where Yahweh was paired with a pagan consort, 'Anat.

From a political point of view the most powerful response came from the exiled Zadokite priests. Theirs was the path of modified pragmatism in the form of accommodation, whereby they collaborated with Persia, which had become the major military power in the Near East after Babylon's fall. They were accordingly favored by the Persians, who supported their return to the land and contributed royal funds to the rebuilding of the temple. They were granted the right to preside over temple and community as long as they offered up prayers on behalf of the Persian king and remained faithful vassals.[5]

Alongside the responses of assimilation, apostasy, and accommodation, there was yet another response, from our perspective the most significant of all. Deriving from a group deprived of power, its immediate effect was slight, though ultimately its influence on the history of ideas outstripped the others. This group's only record consisted of the anonymous outpourings of an apocalyptic vision, leading us to designate its protagonists as "visionaries." According to their vision, Yahweh's purposes for his people had not been fulfilled in Israel's history leading up to the Zadokite theocracy. For their vision of a nation of priests in which the entire people would be righteous (Isa. 60–62) was being contradicted by a hierocratic regime that prevented the masses from having access to God. Moreover, collaboration with the Persian king and a temple built by pagan funds symbolized for them the betrayal of the nation's mission to the world. How dim had become the beacon which was to be "a light to the nations."

The literature in which this group gave expression to their vision represents the dawn of apocalyptic in Israel. It was preserved by somehow becoming attached to other prophetic collections (especially Isaiah 24–27, 56–66, and Zechariah 9–14). Some of the most obscure passages of the Bible are found in this material, material which is not widely read in worship or personal devotion, no doubt in part because of its harsh, disturbing character. Clinging to the old Yahwistic vision of a world in which peace would be wedded with justice, the visionaries looked about them only to witness the flagrant disregard of righteousness by the very leaders who claimed to be Yahweh's holy representatives:

> Therefore justice is far removed from us,
> and righteousness cannot overtake us.
> We look for light, but all is darkness,
> for brightness, but we walk in gloom;
> we grope like blind men for the wall,
> like men without sight we feel our way;
> we stumble at noon as if it were dusk,
> we smell, though healthy men, like dead men;
> we growl like bears, all of us,
> and moan continually like doves;
> we look for justice, but it does not come,
> for salvation, but it is far removed from us.
>   (Isa. 59:9–11)[6]

> Thus justice has turned back
> and righteousness stands far removed,
> for truth has stumbled in the squares
> and uprightness is unable to enter;
> truth is lacking
> and the repentant is robbed.
>   (Isa. 59:14–15a)

Here we recognize a familiar theme of the classical prophets, who were indefatigable in their struggle against perfidy and injustice. But there is a different approach to the theme. Isaiah of Jerusalem, for example, had translated the vision of God's order into concerted political action. In these latter-day visionary followers of Isaiah, however, we encounter the abdication of political action. Not only has truth fallen in the public squares, but there is no legal recourse. The judgment on the present order is total. There no longer being any hope of reform through human agency, the yearning for righteousness flees to a purely transcendent vision of divine intervention:

Then Yahweh saw it with his own eyes
and he realized that there was no one . . .
was appalled that there was no one to intervene.
So *his own arm* brought him victory
and his righteousness upheld him.
He put on righteousness as a breastplate,
the helmet of salvation on his head,
garments of vengeance as his dress,
and he wrapped himself in jealousy as a cloak.
According to deeds he will repay,
wrath to adversaries, due payment to his enemies.
Thus they will fear Yahweh's name from the west,
and his glory from the rising of the sun.
For he will come like a rushing stream
which is driven by the breath of Yahweh;
he will enter into Zion as Redeemer
for those of Jacob who turn from sin.
                                                   (Isa. 59:15b–20)

The creative tension which the prophets had maintained between a vision of God's ideal order and the prophetic vocation of translating that purposeful order into the pragmatics of the sociopolitical realm has dissolved. Weary and defeated, heirs to the prophetic mantle tarry in the vision, for they lack the courage to return to their vocation as servants seeking to awaken human eyes to the path of righteousness. "Truth is lacking, and he who departs from evil makes himself a prey," and so they take refuge instead in a vision of what God will do to vindicate the cause of the oppressed righteous:

For Yahweh is about to come in fire,
and his chariots will be like the hurricane;
to pay back his anger in scorching heat,
and his threat with flames of fire.
For Yahweh will execute judgment with fire,
and with his sword against all flesh,
and those slain by Yahweh will be many.
                                                   (Isa. 66:15–16)

The prophetic perspective had derived from the heavenly vision a plan and a commission: a plan of what God intended with the human family and a commission to integrate into the structures of society God's plan for a peace wedded with justice. We noted that this wedding of vision with pragmatic action was right at home with the classical attitude toward creation in the Bible: God had created this world as a good world, a fitting habitation for humans. The bitter disappointment of the visionaries, which fostered their condemnation of this world as beyond redemption, had a profound effect on their attitude toward the whole created order. No longer was the human vocation construed in terms of integrating vision into the realities of this world so as to restore it to God's intended wholeness. For this world was consigned to doom:

> Behold, the Lord will lay waste the earth and make it desolate,
>   and he will twist its surface and scatter its inhabitants.
>   (Isa. 24:1)

> The earth mourns and withers,
>   the world languishes and withers;
>   the heavens languish together with the earth.
> The earth lies polluted
>   under its inhabitants;
> for they have transgressed the laws,
>   violated the statutes,
>   broken the everlasting covenant.
> Therefore a curse devours the earth,
>   and its inhabitants suffer for their guilt;
> therefore the inhabitants of the earth are scorched,
>   and few people are left.
>   (Isa. 24:4–6)

One aspect of the theology of the prophets is preserved here in the inextricable tie between the anticipated judgment and moral decay. But the vision goes beyond *prophetic* judgment by apparently leaving no room for repentance, and by invoking instead the dualistic imagery of mythology to describe the collapse of the world order into primordial chaos:

> For the windows of heaven are opened,
>   and the foundations of the earth tremble.
> The earth is utterly broken,
>   the earth is rent asunder,
>   the earth is violently shaken.
> The earth staggers like a drunken man,
>   it sways like a hut;
> its transgression lies heavy upon it,
>   and it falls, and will not rise again.
>   (Isa. 24:18c–20)

Hope is not forsaken, however, even in this bleak assessment of reality. But the zeal of the prophets to stir up repentance and to open the nation to God's restoration is abdicated in favor of a more ethereal vision, a purely transcendent solution. The cause of the problem is cosmic, and therefore the solution must be cosmic. The human agency, formerly used by Yahweh, is no longer awaited:

> In that day the Lord with his hard and great and strong sword will punish Leviathan the fleeing serpent, Leviathan the twisting serpent, and he will slay the dragon that is in the sea.
>
> (Isa. 27:1)

> On that day the Lord will punish
>   the host of heaven, in heaven,
>   and the kings of the earth, on the earth.
> They will be gathered together
>   as prisoners in a pit;
> they will be shut up in a prison,
>   and after many days they will be punished.
> Then the moon will be confounded,
>   and the sun ashamed;
> for the Lord of hosts will reign
>   on Mount Zion and in Jerusalem
> and before his elders he will manifest his glory.
>
> (Isa. 24:21–23)

Abdication of the prophetic role of mediation between the heavenly vision and the mundane realities of the community is thus abetted by recourse to the cosmic imagery of myth. This world has become a vale of tears, but the untainted cosmic vision offers a refuge for those weary of human efforts at reform. God will effect the necessary change by taking on the role of divine warrior familiar from cosmogonic myth and defeating both cosmic and earthly enemies of righteousness. "Then Yahweh my God will come, and all the angelic hosts with him" (Zech. 14:5b). The motif which follows the cosmic battle in ancient Near Eastern myth, that of the victory banquet, is applied to portray the salvation which will follow:

> On this mountain the Lord of hosts will make for all peoples a feast of fat things, a feast of wine on the lees, of fat things full of marrow, of wine on the lees well refined. And he will destroy on this mountain the covering that is cast over all . . . nations. He will swallow up death for ever, and the Lord God will wipe away tears from all faces, and the reproach of his people he will take away from all the earth; for the Lord has spoken.
>
> (Isa. 25:6–8)

Since condemnation of the present order is total, and the envisioned destruction of the known world is complete, the positive side of the future vision develops the notion of a new creation:

> For the former troubles will be forgotten,
> they will be hidden from my eyes;
> for now I create new heavens
> and a new earth,
> and the former things will not be remembered,
> nor will they come to mind.
> (Isa. 65:16–17)

> . . . and I shall rejoice over Jerusalem
> and be glad over my people.
> No more will be heard in her the sound of weeping
> or the sound of a cry;
> no more will there be an infant that dies,
> or an old man not living out his days.
> One dying at a hundred will be considered young,
> the sinner dying at a hundred is accursed.
> (Isa. 65:19–20)

> My chosen will not labor in vain,
> they will not bear children for calamity.
> For they shall be a race blessed by Yahweh,
> and their children with them.
> Before they call I shall answer,
> while they are yet speaking I shall have heard.
> The wolf and the lamb will pasture together,
> the lion will eat straw like the ox,
> and dust will be the serpent's food.
> They will do no harm and no destruction
> in all my holy mountain, says Yahweh.
> (Isa. 65:23–25)

The visionaries thus abandon all hope for the existing order, and along with this goes the abdication of half of the prophetic tension, the social and political responsibilities inherent in the prophetic vocation. Even the realm of nature is so fatigued and degenerate that the Noachic order must succumb to a fundamentally new structure:

> On that day there shall be neither heat nor cold (?) nor frost (?). And it shall be continuous day, with no distinction between day and night, and at evening time there shall be light.
> (Zech. 14:6–7)[7]

This brief sketch, covering roughly one century, has traced the development of an apocalyptic perspective out of an earlier prophetic one.[8] In both, the vision of a perfect heavenly order is found, but its function differs sharply. In prophecy the vision is the staging point for a human vocation of deep engagement in the structures of nation and community. In apocalyptic the vision has become a place of refuge from a nation and community so overlaid with corruption and oppression as to become unbearable to world-weary visionaries. Rather than respond to the commission, they choose to linger in the vision; the notion of the importance of human participation in reform is replaced by the passive posture of those awaiting God's total annihilation of the enemy and his creating of a blessed new order.

Inevitably, such a sharp contrast of perspectives raises the question of validity. Should the church endorse the prophetic perspective, with its commitment to reform, or the apocalyptic posture, with its abdication of social engagement? Stated thus, the question itself prompts one to affirm the rightness of the prophetic perspective over the apocalyptic. Such judgment, however, is premature and runs the risk of condemning the apocalyptic perspective before understanding it adequately. Indeed, any evaluation of biblical apocalypticism and any comparisons with contemporary apocalyptic phenomena must take into account the sociopolitical circumstances out of which it arose. To put the matter simply, the visionaries were not afforded the opportunity of freely choosing between the prophetic perspective and that of apocalyptic. Events forced them to choose between a different pair of alternatives, the pragmatic accommodation of the Zadokites or flight into their apocalyptic vision. For they had become a fringe group; they no longer were granted participation in the community whose ways they felt commissioned to reform. They had been excommunicated from the congregation of Israel, their priestly and prophetic offices having been declared null and void. Disenfranchised, they suffered harassment and oppression. Through every hardship, however, they held tenaciously to a vision of divine purpose which was more inclusive than the narrow program of the Zadokites, more egalitarian than the stratified hierocracy which had excluded them, and ultimately more universal in scope. They were instructed to abandon their vision and to contribute servilely to the construction of the Zadokite temple community. But for them to abandon the vision implied forsaking the prophetic heritage to which they had fallen heir, to extinguish "the light to the nations" which they deemed it their responsibility to carry. How could a vision which earthly realities denied them the opportunity of translating into practice be preserved? The visionaries probably had little alternative to withdrawing into the utopian world of the pure, untranslated vision and from there appealing to Yahweh to act:

> Oh, that you would rend the heavens and come down—
> before you the mountains would melt!
> to make known your name to your adversaries—
> before you the nations would tremble!
> as you perform unexpected wonders—
> before you the mountains would melt!
>
> (Isa. 63:19b–64:2)

AN EVALUATION OF
THE APOCALYPTIC RESPONSE
TO LIFE FROM THE PERSPECTIVE OF
THE VISIONARY/PRAGMATIC POLARITY

Against the background of this historical survey of the rise of the apocalyptic perspective out of prophecy, and of the development of the visionary/pragmatic polarity in the Bible, it is possible to return to the problem of distinguishing between that which is faithful and authentically human in apocalypticism and the persistent danger of cowardly escapism. What bearing does the early history of apocalypticism in the Bible have on the questions of faithfulness to God and a healthy knowledge of self? An initial implication is that to be faithful and authentically human means different things in different circumstances. Isaiah of Jerusalem was a respected member of circles close to the king. Being responsible meant something very specific for him. It did not mean being a clever, pragmatic courtier advising the king strictly on the basis of historical experience; nor did it mean being the pure visionary with head so lifted to utopian visions as to disdain the nitty-gritty of politics. For Isaiah, the prestigious Jerusalem leader, being responsible demanded as a mandatory part of his prophetic commission the translation of his vision of God's purpose into the affairs of state.

At a later time, disciples following in the prophetic tradition of Isaiah kept his vision alive, but for them responsibility implied another posture. Bruised, oppressed, and defeated, tottering at the abyss, they needed to withdraw for a time, to heal their wounds in the warmth of a vision unsullied by the bleak realities of their hostile world. Their posture cannot be judged narrowly on the basis of their passivity, for sociopolitical circumstances offered them scarcely an alternative. Rather, the faithfulness and authenticity of their posture can best be evaluated by the response of their descendants in a later day. When this world's realities became more receptive to their vision, did those descendants renew the prophetic vocation? If so, their refuge was in fact a temporary, strategic one, or in words from the poem of Dietrich Bonhoeffer quoted above, a flight from a "victory already achieved"! Among some of their descendants such reengagement in fact occurred, and to those very ones all who count themselves as heirs to the biblical heritage owe their spiritual identity. But also among their descendants were the Gnostics, who became so enraptured by their cosmic vision as to cultivate a disdain for this world. Normal times did not reawaken in them any sense of vocation or social responsibility, and few today would want to count themselves among their descendants. (Of course, the fact that they so despised this world as to give up marriage and childbearing ensured that not many would be counted among their descendants!)

When one seeks to understand apocalyptic movements, ancient and modern, within the context of their particular settings, it is quite natural to find that one's response blends seriousness and sympathy with an element of caution and suspicion. Apocalyptic imagery kept alive a vision of a more perfect order where peace would be wedded with justice for the defeated Jews of ancient times, for beleaguered Europeans of the Middle Ages, for hunted Jews and confessing Christians engulfed by Nazi madness, and for oppressed minorities of our own nation. When we see butterflies painted on prison walls at Dachau, or hear descriptions of paradise in Negro spirituals, for example, we do not criticize the overt passivity of those who thus sketched and sang, but we admire the courageous souls who kept the light of hope aglow by finding refuge in the heavenly vision, for that hope became the springboard for reform when circumstances permitted. Every oppressed person longing to be free must beware, however, of those who would lead their followers, not to an order of peace wedded with justice where God reigns, but to a hell of terror wedded with sadistic authority where a demagogue rules, for Jonestowns rise up in every age as a mockery of the vision of the heavenly Jerusalem.

And Jonestown is but a crass example of a widespread phenomenon. We live in an age where pseudoprophets shout from many pulpits and publish prolifically to exploit and pervert and play upon the insecurities of hollow men and women in a society dedicated to a materialism which cannot satisfy. They tell us: This earth is the late, great planet, now beyond the pale; count the earthquakes, hear the rumors, and step off into my apocalyptic vision. What Daniel envisioned is now coming to pass. Join the elect.

To such apocalypticists, the church and Christian individuals must respond with a plea: Let those suffering Daniel's oppression take refuge in Daniel's vision. His vision, like that of his predecessors, was a refuge for those engulfed by an earthly hell which threatened to snuff out their entire spiritual heritage (not to mention their lives) as the powerful foreign king Antiochus IV tried to draw Jews into the orbit of Hellenism. When faced with stiff resistance, Antiochus apparently did not shy away from persecution, bribery, crucifixion, and other fearsome coercive techniques.

In the biblical understanding of the phenomenon, apocalypticism is not the luxury of the privileged and the comfortable, but the temporary refuge of the afflicted, for whom the world has left no alternative means of keeping faith alive. To those who would bemuse the comfortable with apocalyptic fantasies, Christians should respond no more sympathetically than to those peddling any other medium of escape from responsible engagement in life. We live in a world which has grown bored of every other technique to break the humdrum of sated materialism, and hence it presents a promising field for those who would market apocalypticism as the next thrill for the affluent. For those engulfed by hell, today as in bygone ages, the apocalyptic mode is valid; but for those blessed with the benefits and opportunities of a prosperous, peaceful existence, the Bible commends the more down-to-earth, sober model of the prophetic perspective: Be guided by the vision of the order ordained by God where peace is wedded with justice, but also accept the commission of translating that vision into activity aimed at supplanting world hunger, imperialism, and profiteering with a just, shared prosperity. Incarnate your vision by joining cause with the freedom fighters, the peacemakers, those struggling for human rights, those befriending the lonely and loving the broken in spirit.

This is not to claim that the prosperous of the earth are denied all enjoyment of the images of apocalypticism. They too can fantasize, for the prophetic perspective sets no limits on what God can or may do. Even Isaiah of Jerusalem composed the images, later favored by apocalypticists, of the cow and the bear feeding together and the lion eating straw like the ox, but he *did not let* eschatological fantasies *detract* from his urgent sense of responsibility to incarnate the ideals of justice within the structures of this world. The touchstone of his vocation in the vision indicated that he derived his sense of justice not from a mere extrapolation from existing human possibilities, but from awareness of an ultimate point of reference that guided reality toward a goal which was the property of no human patron. At the same time, the urgency with which he translated that vision into pragmatic action proves that he took seriously what the God of the Exodus took seriously—the events of *this* world as the stage of a divine drama.

There is no denying that the Christian church owes a great deal to its apocalyptic seers of the past, those suffering souls perched precariously at the edge of the abyss and, from that vantage point, peering deeply into aspects of life's mystery which we are inclined to leave unaddressed. They can create in us the capacity to understand the apocalyptic outpourings of the afflicted and oppressed in our own age. Moreover, they prepare us for the encounter with the tempest which we may one day face. And they tear the façade of cold order and efficiency from structures whose underlying decay threatens to engulf us all, though calculating pragmatists and technocrats assure us that our national and world order is secure and in control. But the unholy history of the misuse of apocalypticism warns us as well: let not the harlot of vain, self-centered fantasy detract us from the commission of being faithful to God and authentically human where we are called to live out the human vocation, on this good earth which God created for our mutual enjoyment and care. Here, certainly, the model we derive from our confessional heritage as that appropriate to our time and circumstances is not that of the calculating pragmatist, whether of the secular or of the ecclesiastical variety. But the widespread popularity of that model must not lead Christians to an uncritical appropriation of the visionary model of apocalypticism either. Given the polarity represented by these two extremes and a church being torn apart by "pure" protagonists of each side, we do well to take to heart the tension-filled alternative of Israel's prophets, the art of being in the world yet not of the world, responsible yet not co-opted, engaged yet not coldly efficient in the calculus of worldly pragmatism. We accept our lessons, therefore, from ancient apocalyptic seers. But on ground short of the edge of the abyss we are tutored primarily by the prophets in the courage to be steadfastly and authentically human where the friends of justice are called to live out their lives, namely, within the tension between the vision of an ideal order in which peace is wedded with justice, and the commission to translate that vision into the categories of this world.

Within this tension which comes from our biblical heritage, two authentic sides of faith are kept alive. Here the individual believer and the community of faith, in the absence of the security of a monolithic dogmatic system, center all of existence on the only proper focus of faith, the one true God. This is the radical faith of which Kierkegaard wrote in the book whose title summarizes its thesis: *Purity of Heart Is to Will One Thing.* And it is a faith resting on a security which no earthly power can take away, since no earthly power created or bestowed it in the first place.

Of course we live in a world which places a high premium on security derived from earthly sources. The dominant tone is set by desperate seekers and opportunistic promoters who accentuate those self-centered qualities that provide the subject matter for best sellers these days—self-sufficiency, self-fulfillment, self-confidence. Little wonder that a self-*transcending* posture which commends a life of tension between a vision and a God-given commission fails to win popular support. But Christians have a long history of being called fools, and we in turn should be able to accept the accusation of being "soft" if the tension of faith keeps us somewhat off-balance according to worldly standards; for the grounding of our identity and confidence in God alone allows us to accept a position in life which is both open to God and vulnerable to our fellow human beings. We are able to resist the lure of "pure" systems, religious or secular, with a courage derived from a long, rich spiritual history and that history's witness to the steadfast purposes of a gracious God.

The visionary/pragmatic polarity thus joins the form/reform polarity examined in chapter 2 in fostering an eschatological faith, a faith of openness and self-transcendence. As a narrow, defensive faith is enlarged to receive a richly diverse biblical witness, we rejoice in being able to reclaim the heritage of prophets and seers alike by integrating the poetry of the vision into the prose of the responsible life of faith.

The Twin Polarities
as a *Praeparatio* for the
Messianic Interpretation
of Jesus' Mission

GOD'S ONGOING ACTIVITY INTERPRETED
WITHIN THE POLARITIES OF FAITH

In the previous two chapters, two polarities were described within whose field of tension the faith of Israel developed. Kings and prophets were the representatives of the polarity between form and reform, and their interaction served as a reminder that God's community needed to embrace both the laws and structures which ordered human existence and the ongoing process of reform which challenged and supplanted any structures that became instruments of the privileged in the exploitation of the weak. Seers and their more pragmatic contemporaries drew attention to a related polarity between a vision of a divine order of righteousness and a commitment to translate that vision into the pragmatic realities of the sociopolitical realm. Because of the central confession of biblical faith that God was encountered right in the midst of the historical realm, translation of the vision refined the vision itself, that is, led to a clearer understanding of God's purpose for creation. The *visionary/pragmatic polarity* is equally a *vision/revision polarity*. It remains to be seen how these twin polarities developed in subsequent stages of our confessional heritage, and then to explore what these polarities inherited from kings, prophets, and seers have to say to the contemporary church.

The twin polarities can be represented as shown in figure 1. The form and the vision dimensions have this in common: they seek to embrace reality in its totality on its most fundamental level. The embrace is thus cosmic and tends to be atemporal. The reform and the revision dimensions have a much more directional or teleological thrust.

With a future orientation, they strain toward the fulfillment of divine promises and purposes. Periods of vitality in the Bible have been characterized by balanced interaction between form and reform and between vision and revision. Indeed, the capacity of the faith of Israel to explore cosmos and telos simultaneously is one of its truly noteworthy characteristics.

FIGURE 1

```
                    R
     R              E
     E              V
     F              I
  ←FORM→         ←VISION→
     R              I
     M              O
     ↓              N
                    ↓
```

Stated thus, these polarities may seem quite abstract, though the biblical confessions from which they were extrapolated were not abstract but thoroughly embedded in the stuff of life. In our contemporary setting, the study of these polarities can aid in the theological efforts of the church to grasp the essential qualities and the inner dynamism of the confessions of the Bible. The result can be a more profound understanding of the nature of revelation and a more suitable method of relating a long and diverse confessional heritage to contemporary realities. The polarities that define the field of tension within which the contemporary church is called to respond faithfully are essentially the same ones with which our biblical ancestors struggled. Recognizing this can furnish a valuable historical perspective on difficult problems which tear at the heart of the communities of faith today. Contemporary problems are seen in a new light when understood as manifestations of polarities which have a continuous history over the four thousand years of our tradition, and when it is seen how past generations have discerned within those same polarities an aspect of God's creative, redemptive, purging, and sustaining activity.

As in any aspect of theological study, therefore, it is erroneous to assume that these polarities are to be clarified as ends in themselves, as if biblical theology were aimed solely at analyzing the ontological and metaphysical presuppositions of biblical religion. These conceptual polarities are subservient to a more daring task, that of perceiving the creative, redemptive drama of God as it unfolds over the span of history, and then becoming partners in that drama as it bears all reality toward God's righteous kingdom. A dynamic understanding of biblical revelation thus becomes an invitation to be drawn into the stream which flows steadily through reality and defines the authentic life. Within the confessions with which Israel responded to the events of history, we discern a growth in the understanding of God's purpose. As we relate the vision of God's unfolding kingdom to the events of our time, that growth in understanding continues, and the twin polarities serve to safeguard against one-sided or reductionary interpretations of that purpose. Elsewhere we have sought to underscore the creative tension within this revelatory process of unfolding by describing the manifestation of God occurring within this process as Dynamic Transcendence, that is, as a reality which transcends the human and the mundane and can be glimpsed, as it were, only in the heavenly vision, but which, at the same time, is dynamically involved in the movement of history.[1] Such an understanding calls for constant study of the interaction of our vision of God's purposes with the realities of this world. And it implies ongoing revision and reform as a part of our response to God's gracious activity.

The unfolding of Dynamic Transcendence, however, is not an inexorable process of nature or history. Impersonal models, such as one finds in some versions of process philosophy, inadequately express the biblical vision of reality. In the Bible, reality, understood with historical specificity, is guided toward its goal by a divine Purposer who is not limited to the sum total of the physical substance of the universe and who therefore is best described with personal metaphors like Creator, Redeemer, and Sustainer.

Biblical revelation, as a record of the unfolding of Dynamic Transcendence, is thus a history open to the unexpected and the new. Revelation is not the output of a mechanical generator. It is the manifestation of the activity of One who guides creation according to purpose. This manifestation sometimes takes the form of the inbreaking of the unexpected, sometimes the form of more ordinary events of consolidation and nurture. The confessional heritage is a long record of both types of events, and the church confesses this heritage as a faithful testimony to God's activity on behalf of God's creation.

The ordinary events recorded in the Bible are significant. For example, the attention paid by hymn and proverb to wildlife, winds, stars, and the earth's resources is a reminder that all of creation is a part of God's plan and must be a factor in the faithful community's response. But of special importance are those events in which the community of faith recognized a new, incisive act of God, the inbreaking which supplanted old structures of belief with new understandings. For example, a people living under the oppression of a mythopoeic orthodoxy was encountered by Yahweh, the God who delivers slaves. Or again, a people choking on the dust of brittle doctrines heard God's messenger announcing a new messiah: "Remember not the former things. . . . Behold, I am doing a new thing" (Isa. 43:18–19). We can faithfully grasp the whole unfolding of revelation in the Bible only if we appropriate such paradigms of faith, and that implies reliving them so that the saving history of God's people in the Bible becomes our history. We have a model of such contemporary appropriation in Deut. 5:3, where, five or six centuries after the covenant on Sinai, the people are reminded of the contemporaneousness of the Word of God: "Not with our fathers did the Lord make this covenant, but with us, who are all of us here alive this day." The Passover Seder is another vivid example of the appropriation, or indeed the sacramental reliving, of the saving events of our shared past.

THE SIGNIFICANCE OF THE TWIN POLARITIES INTERPRETED IN THE LIGHT OF THE CHRIST EVENT

This leads to the paradigm which constitutes the heart of the faith of the Christian church. The Christ event is not an isolated event in the history of revelation. It was prepared for by, and cannot be understood apart from, the confessional heritage of the Old Testament. But in the life, death, and resurrection of Jesus Christ, a new breakthrough occurred in God's activity which in its uniqueness still serves as the master paradigm in the Christian's understanding of Dynamic Transcendence. For this reason, the contemporary significance of the twin polarities which developed during the time of kings, prophets, and seers can be grasped by the Christian church only from a perspective which takes into full account the meaning of that master paradigm.

The Form/Reform Polarity in the Early Kerygma

First, we ask, do we find a further unfolding of the king/prophet, or form/reform, polarity in the early kerygma? Here we need to fill in some tradition history from the period of the early monarchy down to the Christian era.

David became for later tradition the model of the ideal king, as one who both assured prosperity and looked after the rights of the widow and orphan. The real-life David failed to measure up to this ideal, and his successors, with few exceptions, failed even more miserably. And thus it was that the prophets battled to keep the reform ingredient of Yahwistic faith alive in active opposition to kings who were devoted to form, that is, devoted to temples, palaces, armies, wealth, and security.

Within the king/prophet polarity the notion of the ideal ruler developed in the direction of messianism. The reason was this: the interaction between kings and prophets kept the ideal alive; yet in real life kings attended to the matters of kings and thereby repeatedly disappointed the hopes of the prophets and their followers. The result was a deferring and finally an eschatologizing of the hope in which the longing for the ideal king was projected into a distant time to come. This encouraged the transformation of the form/reform polarity in the direction of the vision/revision polarity. It is necessary to look more closely at the stages of that transformation.

The king/prophet polarity was brought to a high pitch during the ministry of Isaiah. With solid grounding in the prophetic tradition, Isaiah moved freely within the inside circles of the royal court. He attended to the kingly concerns with form and the prophetic concerns with *re*form. But the interplay between the two abetted a transformation. He could not be satisfied with pragmatic descriptions of the king. It was the *ideal* king which he sought to portray, as seen in Isaiah 9 (on the occasion of Hezekiah's enthronement, perhaps):

> For to us a child is born,
>   to us a son is given;
> and the government will be upon his shoulder,
>   and his name will be called
> "Wonderful Counselor, Mighty God,
>   Everlasting Father, Prince of Peace."
> Of the increase of his government and of peace
>   there will be no end,
> upon the throne of David, and over his kingdom,
>   to establish it, and to uphold it
> with justice and with righteousness
>   from this time forth and for evermore.
> The zeal of the Lord of hosts will do this.
>
> (Isa. 9:6–7)

It is noteworthy in this royal oracle (a genre designed to establish the form dimension of royal ideology) how the standard expressions of royal form are qualified by the reform dimension cultivated by the prophets. See table 1.

TABLE 1	
Form	*Reform*
child born (dynastic principle)	
increase of government and peace: no end	
throne of David	
his kingdom	
establish/uphold . . .	with justice
	with righteousness

This polarity is delineated even more intricately in a closely related composition:

> There shall come forth a shoot from the stump of Jesse,
>   and a branch shall grow out of his roots.
> And the Spirit of the Lord shall rest upon him,
>   the spirit of wisdom and understanding,
>   the spirit of counsel and might,
>   the spirit of knowledge and the fear of the Lord.
> And his delight shall be in the fear of the Lord.

He shall not judge by what his eyes see,
  or decide by what his ears hear;
but with righteousness he shall judge the poor,
  and decide with equity for the meek of the earth;
and he shall smite the earth with the rod of his mouth,
  and with the breath of his lips he shall slay the wicked.
Righteousness shall be the girdle of his waist,
  and faithfulness the girdle of his loins.

The wolf shall dwell with the lamb,
  and the leopard shall lie down with the kid,
and the calf and the lion and the fatling together,
  and a little child shall lead them.
The cow and the bear shall feed;
  their young shall lie down together;
  and the lion shall eat straw like the ox.
The sucking child shall play over the hole of the asp,
  and the weaned child shall put his hand on the adder's den.
They shall not hurt or destroy
  in all my holy mountain;
for the earth shall be full of the knowledge of the Lord
  as the waters cover the sea.

(Isa. 11:1–9)

As in the case of Isaiah 9, we are able to identify the background of Isa. 11:1–9 in the royal psalms. But an important transformation has occurred. Attention has shifted away from the issues at the center of the royal psalms, namely, the glory, universal dominion, and eternal covenant of the Davidic king. Emphasis falls instead on the responsibility of the ideal ruler to uphold righteousness and equity.[2] This change in emphasis is the result of the impregnation of royal oracle with the reform dynamic of prophetic Yahwism. The balance achieved is noteworthy, and the tension thereby effected is of great theological significance. See table 2.

The old reform ideals, dating all the way back to the League period, thus were kept alive by being drawn *into* a picture of the ideal king. For several centuries the prophets struggled to hold together the qualities of form and reform in Israel. In this effort they were able to utilize the ancient metaphor of king as shepherd, a metaphor connoting strength combined with care for the weak (for example, Ezekiel 34). To be sure, most of the Davidic kings were woefully lacking in the ideal character-

Form	Reform
shoot of Jesse/branch	spirit of the Lord
wisdom	counsel
understanding	might
knowledge	fear of the Lord
faithfulness	judge with righteousness
(description of peace and prosperity)	decide with equity
	smite the earth
	slay the wicked

TABLE 2

istics. Realities did not lead the prophets to abandon the ideal, however. Instead, they continued to interpret history as the arena of God's activity, and events thus led them to revise and refine the messianic ideal. And when it was denied expression in real life, they kept the ideal alive by *projecting it into the future* and thus awaiting the messiah whom God would finally send to lead his people in righteousness. Within the world view nurtured by the prophets, the function earlier exercised by a rather static notion of form was being replaced by the dynamic notion of a vision open to revision on the basis of God's ongoing activity in the life of the nation and the world.

Fervent Yahwists believed that upon the enthronement of Josiah in 640 B.C. God's chosen Davidic messiah had finally arrived. The exuberant commentators of the time could report, "Before him there was no king like him, who turned to the Lord with all his heart and with all his soul and with all his might, according to all the law of Moses; nor did any like him arise after him" (2 Kings 23:25). Josiah seemed to embody all the characteristics of the messianic ideal, as that ideal had developed up to that time. He was pious and observant of Israel's covenant with Yahweh, he was just, and he was gloriously triumphant in defeating Israel's enemies, expanding the nation's borders to rival David's empire, and bringing in wealth through trade and conquest. But was this the kind of messiah who would lead the nation back to a full commitment to God? The discouraging history of failure accumulated by the dazzling warrior kings of the Davidic house led some Yahwists to be skeptical. Jeremiah, for one, was conspicuously silent during the heights of Josiah's reform and royal power. Covenant by compulsion and kingdom by military might seemed contrary to the heart of Israel's faith. To Jeremiah came Yahweh's promise of a new initiative, a new covenant, unlike the old, with the Torah being written upon the heart:

> Behold, the days are coming, says the Lord, when I will make a new covenant with the house of Israel and the house of Judah, not like the covenant which I made with their fathers when I took them by the hand to bring them out of the land of Egypt, my covenant which they broke, though I was their husband, says the Lord. But this is the covenant which I will make with the house of Israel after those days, says the Lord: I will put my law within them, and I will write it upon their hearts; and I will be their God, and they shall be my people. And no longer shall each man teach his neighbor and teach his brother, saying, 'Know the Lord,' for they shall all know me, from the least of them to the greatest, says the Lord; for I will forgive their iniquity, and I will remember their sin no more.
>
> (Jer. 31:31–34)

The inadequacy of the messianic ideal of the dazzling, conquering king was driven home to the people of Judah in a chain of harsh lessons from history: In 609 Josiah was struck down in battle by Pharaoh Neco II, thereby nullifying in one cruel blow the lofty messianic expectations which had been attached to this Davidic king. A series of vain, weak kings succeeded him as the nation tumbled headlong toward disaster. The Babylonians conquered the land in 587, which resulted in devastation of the city, burning of the temple, and further deportation.

In chapter 3 reference was made to the varied responses which came from the broken nation. Here we simply note that once again the manifestation of God's purpose was recognized by the most perceptive of the people, and this time it implied a harsh indictment of the popular notions of what it meant to be God's people and God's anointed ruler. Peoplehood had come to be associated with glory, with lording it over the other nations, even as the anointed ruler was conceived of as a dazzling potentate who would lead the people to victory over their enemies. As a result of the destruction of nation and temple, God's servants, the prophets, began to unfold a mystery: God had not abandoned his people, but he had demonstrated a very different ideal of peoplehood and leadership. The most profound formulation of this revised ideal stems from the anonymous prophet we call Second Isaiah. The royal messiah, the victorious conquering one, would actually be a pagan, the Persian Cyrus. He would be Yahweh's agent in restoring the people to their land. But in place of the royal Davidic messiah, a different ideal is described for the indigenous leadership of the nation, that of the suffering servant. The abortion of the old ideal miraculously led to the birth of the notion of a leader who draws the people to God not through force of arms but through the gentle administration of justice, through acts of healing, through compassion and even bitter personal suffering. And a suffering-servant leader implied a suffering-servant role for the nation as well:

> Behold my servant, whom I uphold,
>   my chosen, in whom my soul delights;
> I have put my Spirit upon him,
>   he will bring forth justice to the nations.
> He will not cry or lift up his voice,
>   or make it heard in the street;
> a bruised reed he will not break,
>   and a dimly burning wick he will not quench;
>   he will faithfully bring forth justice.
> He will not fail or be discouraged
>   till he has established justice in the earth;
>   and the coastlands wait for his law.
>
> Thus says God, the Lord,
>   who created the heavens and stretched them out,
>   who spread forth the earth and what comes from it,
> who gives breath to the people upon it
>   and spirit to those who walk in it:
> "I am the Lord, I have called you in righteousness,
>   I have taken you by the hand and kept you;
> I have given you as a covenant to the people,
>   a light to the nations,
>   to open the eyes that are blind,
> to bring out the prisoners from the dungeon,
>   from the prison those who sit in darkness.
>   (Isa. 42:1–7)

This ideal not only replaced might with suffering compassion, but it took the focus off one exalted ruler and democratized the ideal to apply to all the righteous in the nation. And beyond this, it broke nationalistic restraints:

[The Lord] says:
"It is too light a thing that you should be my servant
   to raise up the tribes of Jacob
   and to restore the preserved of Israel;
I will give you as a light to the nations,
   that my salvation may reach to the end of the earth."
                                                    (Isa. 49:6)

The startling new ideal was formulated most sublimely in the fourth
of the so-called suffering-servant songs, found in Isa. 52:13—53:12:

Behold, my servant shall prosper,
   he shall be exalted and lifted up,
   and shall be very high.
As many were astonished at him—
   his appearance was so marred, beyond human semblance,
   and his form beyond that of the sons of men—
so shall he startle many nations;
   kings shall shut their mouths because of him;
for that which has not been told them they shall see,
   and that which they have not heard they shall understand.
                                                (Isa. 52:13–15)

The manner in which the servant will shock nations into astonished
recognition of God's righteousness is so new that Second Isaiah's words
seem to surpass his own understanding. They are thus pregnant with a
significance which would become clear to the people only centuries
later, as a result of God's new act in Jesus Christ:

Surely he has borne our griefs
   and carried our sorrows;
yet we esteemed him stricken,
   smitten by God, and afflicted.
But he was wounded for our transgressions,
   he was bruised for our iniquities;
upon him was the chastisement that made us whole,
   and with his stripes we are healed.
All we like sheep have gone astray;
   we have turned every one to his own way;
and the Lord has laid on him
   the iniquity of us all.
                                                (Isa. 53:4–6)

Having traced the essential lines of development of the ideal of king, it is now possible to return to the question of the relation between the ideals of king and prophet in the master paradigm of our faith, the gospel of Jesus Christ. In seeking to grasp the nature and significance of Jesus of Nazareth, the early church placed him in a line of continuity with the kings of the house of David, as indicated by the genealogies in Matthew 1 and Luke 3. Connection is made with Isaiah's messianic ideal in the birth narrative in Matthew:

> Behold, a virgin shall conceive and bear a son,
> and his name shall be called Emmanuel.
>   (Matt. 1:23, referring to Isa. 7:14)

This connection is strengthened by the entry narrative in all four Gospels, according to which Jesus, mounted upon the traditional beast of royalty, the ass, is greeted as a king: "Hosanna to the Son of David!" (Matt. 21:9). Matthew and John further tighten the connection between Jesus and the messianic ideal by quoting Zech. 9:9:

> Tell the daughter of Zion,
> Behold, your king is coming to you,
> humble, and mounted on an ass,
> and on a colt, the foal of an ass.
>   (Matt. 21:5)

But what kind of royal or messianic ideal does this king fulfill? In Matthew the crowds report, "This is the *prophet* Jesus from Nazareth of Galilee" (Matt. 21:11, emphasis added). One can readily understand how this uncommon preacher of righteousness, who spoke out courageously against hypocrisy and wickedness without regard for stature or power, would be called a prophet. But he was not simply a prophet, either, as the contrast between John the Baptist and Jesus indicates. Yes, he drove out the money-changers and attacked the Pharisees, but he also recognized Caesar's due (Matt. 22:15–22). It becomes apparent that in Jesus there occurred a radically new embodiment of the king/prophet polarity. And as these traditional earthly vehicles of divine revelation were taken up in a new way in Jesus' life, the delicate balance between form and reform received yet another transformation, this one more profound than any which had come earlier.

Luke placed Jesus' mission within the context of the activity of God described in the song of Hannah by including the Magnificat in the introduction of his Gospel:

He has shown strength with his arm,
he has scattered the proud in the imagination of their hearts,
he has put down the mighty from their thrones,
and exalted those of low degree;
he has filled the hungry with good things,
and the rich he has sent empty away.
He has helped his servant Israel,
in remembrance of his mercy,
as he spoke to our fathers,
to Abraham and to his posterity for ever.

(Luke 1:51–55)

That is to say, Jesus carried forward the redemptive work of Yahweh, inaugurated long ago when Hebrew slaves were delivered from Egyptian kings. And this reform dynamic reverberates throughout the ministry of Jesus, whose life energy was dedicated to freeing humans from the many forms of bondage which held them, whether imposed by self or by others. Simultaneously this prophetic reformer was also the righteous king, attending to the needs of people for sustenance and succor. Therefore, in the same first chapter of Luke, we read Zechariah's words:

Blessed be the Lord God of Israel,
for he has visited and redeemed his people,
and has raised up a horn of salvation for us
in the house of his servant David.

(Luke 1:68–69)

The royal designation of Jesus is expressed powerfully in the seventh chapter of Luke by application of another Old Testament tradition. In verses 24–27 Jesus identifies John with the messenger Elijah of Mal. 3:1 and 4:5; this constitutes unambiguous confession of the messianic claims of Jesus.

Jesus was able to incarnate the two ideals of king and of prophet by fulfilling the mission of the suffering servant, that is to say, by being anointed into God's service by tears of anguish, by taking "upon himself the chastisement that made us whole." Perhaps one comes closest to Jesus' own self-understanding in the imagery of the suffering servant. But aside from what may be surmised about Jesus' self-consciousness, it is clear that the early church was convinced that in Jesus the office of the suffering servant had found its messianic incumbent:

And he came to Nazareth, where he had been brought up; and he went
to the synagogue, as his custom was, on the sabbath day. And he stood
up to read; and there was given to him the book of the prophet Isaiah.
He opened the book and found the place where it was written,
"The Spirit of the Lord is upon me,
because he has anointed me to preach good news to the poor.
He has sent me to proclaim release to the captives
and recovering of sight to the blind,
to set at liberty those who are oppressed,
to proclaim the acceptable year of the Lord."
And he closed the book, and gave it back to the attendant, and sat down;
and the eyes of all in the synagogue were fixed on him. And he began
to say to them, "Today this scripture has been fulfilled in your hearing."
(Luke 4:16–21)

Luke's Gospel prompts an understanding of Jesus as fulfiller of the
king/prophet polarity also by including this account of a query from
John:

The disciples of John told him of all these things. And John, calling
to him two of his disciples, sent them to the Lord, saying, "Are you he
who is to come, or shall we look for another?" And when the men had
come to him, they said, "John the Baptist has sent us to you, saying,
'Are you he who is to come, or shall we look for another?' "
(Luke 7:18–20)

Is this Jesus the long-awaited one, the messiah of God, "he who comes"?
Jesus does not reply, "Go and tell John that I am the king of the house
of David, here to restore the kingdom of Israel." This would have been
too one-sided an affirmation of form. His answer instead once again
grafted into the ideal of king the ideal of prophet:

And he answered them, "Go and tell John what you have seen and
heard: the blind receive their sight, the lame walk, lepers are cleansed,
and the deaf hear, the dead are raised up, the poor have good news
preached to them. And blessed is he who takes no offense at me."
(Luke 7:22–23)

The annals of history of course indicate that those who did take offense at such a humble king were many. Among his own followers there
have never been lacking powerful voices encouraging the triumphalistic
interpretation of his messianic office. This is an interpretation which the
masses find very attractive, as they yearn for a religion which will sanc-
tify their greed and lust for power; thus they scan the horizon for a

glorious messiah who will lead them to victory over their enemies rather than reconciliation, to lordship over the peoples rather than suffering service. The temptation perennially facing the church of trying to satisfy this yearning is indeed powerful and has often led to a crippling of the church's effectiveness.

It is clear from these passages in Luke, however, that Jesus was interpreted as the messiah in a particular way which eschews conventional pictures of earthly power. This unique interpretation was in part due to the careful balancing of royal and prophetic qualities, but it was especially the result of the identification of Jesus with the figure of the suffering servant. This means that the mission of Jesus and its significance for the church cannot be understood apart from the long *praeparatio* found in the Old Testament. God's people had never given up the expectation of a messiah chosen by God who would one day come to establish among them a kingdom wedding peace with righteousness. They persevered in this hope in spite of repeated disappointments. Indeed, those very disappointments, that long history of one messiah after the other failing God and people through self-service, led to the unfolding of a messianic ideal which culminated in Christ's accepting the mission of the suffering servant as his own.

At the same time as we acknowledge this continuity with the past, we must also recognize that in the Christ event we have the most vivid example in the Bible of the other aspect of Dynamic Transcendence, the encounter with the new act of God which casts all that preceded in a new light. Here is a prime instance of the phenomenon encountered by Second Isaiah:

> Remember not the former things,
>   nor consider the things of old.
> Behold, I am doing a new thing;
>   now it springs forth, do you not perceive it?
>   (Isa. 43:18–19b)

Those whose system was definitive and closed, who felt that God's previous acts had closed the book on theological understanding, could only take offense at a *suffering* messiah. Those standing within the vision/revision polarity, however, were open to the possibility of the radically new act of God.[3] And among those characterized by this eschatological openness, a sublime secret was unveiled: Finally, following one disappointment after the other, the Messiah had come who did not disappoint. He proved his election not by collecting powerful armies, amassing wealth, and building palaces (monuments vulnerable to destruction and decay) but by restoring the sick and preaching to the poor the good news of the inbreaking of God's kingdom. The messianic promises of the Old Covenant were thereby fulfilled in the embodiment of the kingship/prophecy ideals in Jesus of Nazareth. And true to the vision/revision polarity, in this most thorough translation of the vision, the older vision was revised in such a profound manner that we recognize in the Christ event the master paradigm of our faith. Here we encounter the act of God which more than any other reveals to us God's purpose with us and our world.

In Jesus the messianic hope, which had been given clear focus by Isaiah and had been enriched by Second Isaiah, was fulfilled: here, finally, was Immanuel, "God with us." And this gracious act of "God with us" even went beyond the suffering-servant image of Second Isaiah: here was God's Messiah, God's anointed Son; the suffering which atones was no longer assigned to a prophet but was taken on by the Messiah, and thus by God. Royal messiah and suffering prophet were thereby united. This union of *ruling king* and *suffering prophet* is drawn together in the Letter to the Hebrews with the third major office of Hebrew antiquity, that of *priest*. Christ, through his suffering, has become our High Priest, and in that office he mediates to us the new covenant spoken of by Jeremiah, the laws of which are written on the hearts of the people. The author of the Letter to the Hebrews summarizes the point well: "In many and various ways God spoke . . . to our fathers by the prophets; but in these last days he has spoken to us by a Son" (1:1–2a).

The Vision/Revision Polarity in the Early Kerygma

These few examples from the New Testament illustrate how the king/prophet, or form/reform, polarity was embodied and fulfilled in Jesus Christ. We have already made reference to the embodiment of the vision/revision polarity but shall here add several specific points. Once again there is no question that Jesus' vision of God's kingdom was based solidly on his Hebrew tradition: when asked to identify the heart of the Torah, he pointed to the love of God and the love of neighbor, thereby drawing upon biblical tradition and combining these two elements in the manner of rabbis contemporary with him (Matt. 23:34-40 and parallels). But never before had the vision of the kingdom received such *complete* translation into the realities of this world. Never before, that is to say, had divine purpose and the will of a human drawn together into such a thorough bonding at a crucial juncture in the history of God's relating to the human family. Thus the vision of the fulfillment of the intent of the old covenant in a new covenant was realized in Jesus through such thorough translation of that vision that the early followers found the confessional language of incarnation to be the most adequate means of describing God's new activity. The vision/revision polarity, which speaks of the unfolding of the vision precisely in its translation, prepares us to discern the most remarkable revision of all the biblical visions precisely in that preeminent of all translations, the incarnation. The tension between vision and revision is vividly illustrated by the Sermon on the Mount:

> Think not that I have come to abolish the law and the prophets; I have come not to abolish them but to fulfil them. For truly, I say to you, till heaven and earth pass away, not an iota, not a dot, will pass from the law until all is accomplished. Whoever then relaxes one of the least of these commandments and teaches men so, shall be called least in the kingdom of heaven; but he who does them and teaches them shall be called great in the kingdom of heaven. For I tell you, unless your right-eousness exceeds that of the scribes and Pharisees, you will never enter the kingdom of heaven.
>
> (Matt. 5:17-20)

Once the lines of continuity with the traditional notion of Torah have thus been secured, Jesus goes on to the radical revision implied by his application of the heart of the Torah to life:

> You have heard that it was said to the men of old, "You shall not kill; and whoever kills shall be liable to judgment." But I say to you that every one who is angry with his brother shall be liable to judgment; whoever insults his brother shall be liable to the council, and whoever says, "You fool!" shall be liable to the hell of fire.
>
> (Matt. 5:21-22)

> You have heard that it was said, "You shall not commit adultery." But I say to you that every one who looks at a woman lustfully has already committed adultery with her in his heart.
>
> (Matt. 5:27-28)

Life within the vision/revision polarity was for Christ a life of stress, but it was the kind of stress which was open to the inbreaking of God's kingdom. For the Kingdom of God was in the world, though not of the world. It was transcendent, while furnishing the very direction and purpose that guides every earthly reality. The source of the tension between realized and futuristic eschatology is thus at the heart of the kerygma, indeed, at the heart of the teaching of the kingdom by Jesus himself. Hence it is the task of Christian theology not to dissolve it in favor of one side or the other but to preserve it so as to place life at the heart of the tension of eschatological faith.

There are other aspects of both polarities which could be explored, for example, the delicate balancing found in the New Testament between the cosmic thrust of the form dimension and the teleological thrust of the reform dimension. The enduring, almost timeless quality of the form dimension is expressed in the *logos* tradition incorporated in the prologue to the Gospel of John, as it is in the notion of the cosmic Christ of Colossians and the High Priest "after the order of Melchizedek" in the Letter to the Hebrews. And much could be said about the vision/revision polarity after careful study of the apocalyptic dimension within the New Testament. But such study remains to be done.

THE EMBODIMENT OF THE TWIN POLARITIES
BY THE CHURCH

Even as each stage in the history of the polarities we have been examining prepared for the next stage of their development, the dynamic process continues beyond the history of biblical confessions. The images of king, prophet, and seer were unified in Christ not to end the history of their interaction but to open new and richer avenues of development. Not only did the Messiah of the house of David, Jesus the Christ, startle his disciples by instructing them in the suffering which awaited *him* upon his entry into his royal city, but he went on to explain, "If any man would come after me, let him deny himself and take up his cross and follow me" (Matt. 16:24). The path of the master is to be the path of his followers, and that path is the way of the cross.

The church proclaims that the incarnate One is still present in the world, for those gathered in Christ's name and drawn into God's purposes *are* the body of Christ in the world, as the Apostle Paul pointed out to the Corinthians. This means that the king/prophet polarity embodied by Christ must continue to find embodiment in the church. It means as well that the vision/revision dialectic still prods the church to place its efforts behind the faithful translation of the vision of the Kingdom of God into the pragmatic realities of this world. The forms of Christianity which have been capable of adapting to ever-new contexts without sacrificing the dynamic substance of biblical faith have been able to do so in no small part through preservation of these polarities.

Of course, the implications of the applicability of the form/reform and vision/revision polarities to the life of today are multivalent and often complex. In any case, care is always necessary in attending to the twin tasks of clearly formulating the vision which draws God's people toward a more humane and just future and of courageously embodying that vision in the concrete realities of life. Similarly in need of balanced attention are the preservation of dependable forms that are capable of ordering and supporting life, and the exercise of the type of prophetic reform which embraces the struggle of the weak and the poor against oppressive structures.

In the next two chapters examples of these tasks will be explored. Chapter 5 will focus on the challenge facing the church of effectively appropriating the vision of its confessional heritage and reformulating and revitalizing it in creative new metaphors. Chapter 6 will turn from interpretation of the heritage to the mandate to respond by translating the vision of God's kingdom received from tradition into the needs and challenges of this world, and to do so in imitation of the incarnate Christ, that is, by the way of the cross.

In this task of balancing and translating, the twin polarities we have described may aid us in grasping more adequately several fundamental characteristics of our faith. As an eschatological faith, which was born of God's past gracious acts but also awaits God's new acts in times to come, we live expectantly between the realized and the not-yet-accomplished. This expectancy creates an openness which is essential to faith, an openness which maintains a vulnerability to God's initiative, a sensitivity to God's word spoken through God's prophets. It protects us from the lure of triumphalism, the path of the dazzling messiahs who drive all opponents to submission through displays of power and who exalt their followers to be princes over the rest of the human family rather than call them to compassionate and, if need be, suffering service.

These twin polarities, by cautioning against a closed theological system and a facile "naming of the whirlwind,"[4] help safeguard an aspect of God felt so awesomely by the saints of all ages but ignored by opportunistic ecclesiasts: the hiddenness of God.[5] God is not one object alongside others, to be examined and described. We do not hold Yahweh in a yoke. We are called rather into the service of one whose aura of holiness is not dissolved. Therefore, we serve obediently within a field of tension which keeps us open to God's mystery, aware of our own unworthiness, receptive to the *sola gratia,* sensitive to the faithful response of others, eager for growth in fellowship, and sustained by the vision of the kingdom to come.

CHAPTER 5

The Faithful Response (1)

The Interpretation and Transformation of Biblical Symbols

THE BEARING OF THE TWIN POLARITIES ON RELIGIOUS SYMBOLISM

That words are able to communicate a dynamic reality which draws humans into a creative, redemptive process embracing all of history and the entire human family is a daring claim. Yet that is the claim which Christians make for the Word which they have received in their scriptural heritage. We have already noted, however, that Christians are not immune to the temptation of trying to circumscribe that Word, to specify the segment of humanity to which it applies, and to set limits on the period of time in which the Word of God unfolded new chapters of meaning. Resisting this tendency to "domesticate" God's Word, we have discerned in the Bible polarities that preserve a human condition of openness within which the creative, redemptive reality that moved so dynamically through biblical history can continue to move today. Those polarities function in relation to various specific tasks facing the church, including the task of giving expression to God's presence and activity in appropriate symbols.

As in the case of the writings of Scripture generally, so too in the case of symbols and images, vehicles capable of giving powerful expression to the dynamic reality at the heart of Scripture can be encapsulated within human constructions that render them impotent. Recently Blacks, women, and reform leaders of the so-called third world have subjected traditional symbolism and the contemporary use of symbolism to close scrutiny. They have drawn attention not only to the impotence of many of our symbols but also to the destructive effects which the unfaithful use of symbolism can have on oppressed human beings. Hence it seems urgent that efforts to grasp the inner dynamic of our biblical and confessional heritage address the question of the present crisis in traditional symbolism and imagery. For the hallowed words of our heritage are ill-suited to communicate Dynamic Transcendence if they evoke primarily feelings of hostility and alienation in their hearers.

This crisis is felt even in our most cherished hymns and prayers. For example, it would be revealing to discover what range of feelings are evoked in our congregations as these words are prayed: "Our *Father* who are in heaven, hallowed by thy name. Thy *kingdom* come . . ."

Symbols, those stained-glass windows through which mortals peer, hoping to glimpse the holy center of life, have shattered before the eyes of many Christians. Images that breathed serenity and concord into communities of belief for ages lie broken on chancel floors in the path of angry mobs of iconoclasts, who destroy in the name of their particular causes.

Heavenly Father, Divine Warrior, Glorious King, rallying calls of countless generations of the faithful, not only cause pain for some as sounding gongs and clashing symbols but have become a *scandalon* over which others have stumbled and become badly bruised. Only haltingly do they pray, only privately do they pick up the old vessels in moments of longing and nostalgia. Are we not well-advised, then, by radical theologians to discard such objects of discord, stop peering into the cathedral of transcendence, turn instead to the asphalt and concrete slabs of life unencumbered by names for the Holy?

History teaches us the futility of attempts to supplant the sense of mystery fostered by symbolism with a purely rationalistic pragmatism. We have witnessed time and again how communities have swept their sanctuaries free of symbols, removed the leaded panes, dismantled the holy pillars, to stand staring at life with the naked eye of autonomous *humanum*. And after a period of headstrong celebration of the human center, that paragon of truth and beauty, the ceremony ends not with a hymn to the secular spirit but with "the rumor of angels."[1] The concrete slab does not seem to manifest a center, a frame upon which to hang the banners of human experience. And the peering begins anew. The sense of a mysterious source, which has something essential to contribute to the quality of life on the concrete slab, leads to the renewal of attempts to name the whirlwind, describe the mystery, discover whether it is good and dependable, whether it empowers the defenseless or simply defends the empowered.

Few therefore will dispute the importance, perhaps even the inevitability, of images and symbols in religious experience and communal existence. Symbols allow us to approach the Holy with awe and earnestness and yet with the dash of mirth which keeps us on the mortal side of the iconostasis. But symbols and images, those windows of transcendence, have become a source of dissension within the church.

For instance, only after centuries of tentative probing and growth in understanding did a biblical community find itself addressing God with the intimate word *abba*, "father." The Jewish society within which that image grew clothed the concept of fatherhood with connotations of awe, protection, tender love, and trustworthiness. How different is the experience of many in our society, to whom father is a symbol of either absence or indifference, and whose hurtful contact with males in later life develops it further into a sign of demeaning authority and repressive power. To pray to a heavenly Father is for them a distressing experience, though for others it remains profoundly meaningful.

In other instances, within the same sanctuary God the Warrior is for one group an image of hope that one day the oppressor will fall and, for another group, a specter of aggrandizing imperialism. Never shall I forget my late colleague G. Ernest Wright, booming forth in his inimitable style against the nascent peace movement of the mid-sixties: "Yahweh the Warrior was no pacifist, nor am I!" We remember well that troubled period when an image which represented, for some, a summons to defend a holy cause conjured up the terrible specter in the minds of others of shining belt buckles inscribed, *Gott mit uns.* As a college counselor I remember leading campfire groups in the spirited singing of "Stand Up, Stand Up for Jesus." Recently in worship I could not make it past the words "Lift high his royal banner; It must not suffer loss. / From vict'ry unto vict'ry / His army shall he lead, / Till ev'ry foe is vanquished / And Christ is Lord indeed." Sounding gongs and clashing symbols!

If the discord were mainly a matter of differing aesthetic tastes, we should merely make our choice and give the matter no further thought. But religious symbols are not like so many literary allusions in a poem by Ezra Pound, or like a torn glove to be removed and discarded, or a broken chalice to be replaced. The vessel has intermingled with the meaning it has carried for centuries; in the minds of many, for example, God and Father cannot be separated without pain and loss. Even if nostalgia and custom were the only factors, our problem would be relatively simple. But the matter goes deeper. In the practice of the church and the individual, symbols are drawn into the use and abuse of *power*. Symbols are used to direct the attention of foundering moderns to a transcendent meaning which holds promise of breaking their bonds of alienation and futility. Symbols are also used to reinforce the status of inferiority and powerlessness that has been imputed to certain groups within the church. In a word, symbols are used *both* to defend the empowered and to empower the defenseless.

Let us turn to four examples of the battle over symbols and images, and the models of leadership they imply. First, we are all familiar with hymns and liturgical prayers which portray God as light and the giver of light. "Light of light, enlighten me, / Now anew the day is dawning; / Sun of grace, the shadows flee, / Brighten thou my Sabbath morning; / With Thy joyous sunshine blest, / Happy is my day of rest!" The night of history is past, we have left the darkness. The Judge has become a gracious Savior. "Break forth, O beauteous heavenly light, / And usher in the morning." Those who perceive life as darkness are admonished to see the silver lining, lest their outlook betray their lack of faith. Amid such "light"-hearted Christians there wanders a Jew with a story to tell, of a Christian culture turned mad, of a people gassed in ovens, of a world God seems to have abandoned, a story not of day and light but of darkness and Night! Our triumphalist songs and liturgies crackle like the brittle plaster of frescoes prematurely exposed to the heat. Thus Elie Wiesel arrests our attention as he portrays the Night which we feared as children but have subsequently tried to convince ourselves no longer threatens us in adulthood. W. H. Auden describes our plight: "Lost in a haunted wood, children afraid of the night, who have never been happy or good."[2] Douglas Hall reinforces these reminders of a symbol we prefer to ignore as he portrays darkness and insists that until we see the darkness, we shall fail to see the light.[3]

As the Judeo-Christian tradition cannot look at its images and symbols in the same light "after Auschwitz," neither can it look at God the Father in the same way after Mary Daly and Rosemary Ruether. To be sure, long before Daly and Ruether, many women of a more silent sort suffered antigospel under the tyranny of males who were holding them securely in their allotted positions within a universe sponsored by a cosmic Patriarch and *his* high priests. But these women *documented* the oppression in terms untamed by the customary female proprieties. Men squirmed uneasily, and a church still squirms over the question of what lies beyond God the Father.

Add to this the impact of James Cone as he called into question the white Jesus with whom the empowered felt comfortable at their afternoon sherry, and spoke instead of a black Jesus, an eschatological preacher proclaiming a day of judgment on those at ease and a day of release for slaves and captives. The attempts to draw up scholarly briefs to prove the unhistorical basis of Cone's conclusions have not disguised the underlying fears of white exploiters that their bluff has been called by the very ones they depended on to cater to them in unquestioning servitude. A whole lovely life, deriving holy blessing from the church, was being called into question in the name of a godly, *righteous* love which exposed the pampering, *paternalistic* love of many Christians as a noisy gong and a clanging symbol.

The patron God in stars and stripes was the next to come under fire, the patron of the "one nation, under God." And the attack came from all sides this time, from analysts exposing the idolatry of civil religion, from Marxist Christians uncovering the imperialistic capitalism of a Marcionite gospel, and from conservationists critical of God the National Developer.

God of light, Father God, white Jesus, patron God, all cracking under the hammer blows of virulent criticism. What is happening here? Do we witness another sign of the decline of the church? Conflict of the magnitude we have described certainly can shatter and destroy, and can lead the critics of traditional symbols to seek out alternative communities more sympathetic to their vision. But iconoclasm has been an essential part of our heritage from the time of the prophets, and of necessity. For much symbolism and imagery has little to do with the one true God, but instead seeks to clothe God in garments dulling divine splendor to the pastel tones of bourgeois taste. Thus the attempts to co-opt God by enlisting him as patron of number one, the country whose GNP must grow every year and whose international preeminence is deemed the necessary sign of divine favor, are no less a blatant form of idolatry than the attempts of Israelite kings to control God by housing the ark in a royal chapel. And the white Jesus with the blond curls, smiling on prosperity won at the cost of third-world poverty, is no different from the Aryan face reflected back from the well of the life-of-Jesus researchers of Adolf von Harnack's era.[4] Some images and symbols are plainly and simply idolatrous, and any living religious community must heed the voices of its prophetic iconoclasts and reformers.

But are not iconoclasts predisposed to carry their demolition too far? How about God the Father and God of light? Do the problems these symbols raise justify casting them out with the white Jesus and the God in stars and stripes? We must be discriminating here, recalling first of all that *all* images of God participate in idolatry; nor should we be too hasty in excepting *verbal* images. For any attempt to name the ineffable One brings the mortal close to hubris. It is a natural trait of God-lovers, however, to desire to name the object of their devotion, and thus Jesus named God *Abba,* and Johannine tradition named God Light. Because of that naming, have these images become a permanent part of our tradition? Or are they vessels that have served their purpose and can now be replaced by images born of new experience?

These questions emerge from the heart of the form/reform and vision/revision polarities and remind us that the vision we have inherited from our confessional past must not be mindlessly repeated but must be given new life through embodiment in the Christian community. Since authentic application of the vision implies revision, and since every form must be accompanied by reform, we best approach the reappropriation, reformulation, and transformation of symbols in light of their origin and function in the dramatic history of the growth of biblical tradition.

THE FUNCTION OF SYMBOLS AND IMAGES IN THE BIBLE

Ancient Israel faced the challenge which modern developments have thrust upon us once again, that of naming the whirlwind, describing the center, conceptualizing what is utterly essential for the grounding and ordering of individual and communal life. Israelites looked where we look for hints—to their experiences, which they interpreted against the background of a confessional heritage. In history, patterns emerged that seemed to be descriptive of the unfolding of a purposeful movement through space and time. Certain events seemed to manifest with special clarity the inner dynamic of that movement. In the history of confessions in the Bible, we thus observe a development from events to mettonymies, to symbols, to sacraments, and, finally, as the most abstract level of inference, to images of God. In the case of the first foundational event of Israel, we witness a complex web of realities and events experienced by Hebrew slaves, see the confession then focus on deliverance at the Red Sea, witness the emergence of the symbol of parting waters, the sacramental development of the Seder, and finally the emergence of a powerful image of God as Deliverer of the oppressed.

No one event, symbol, or image, however, became the exclusive, immutable representative of Hebrew faith. The old "namings" were repeatedly related to new experiences in the life of the people, and a dynamic process of growth occurred which included the growth of symbols and images. On the level of images, we witness how God in the settlement was experienced as Sustainer, in the struggle with Baalism as Creator, in the monarchy as universal King, in the cult as Holy of Holies, in the conflict with powerful corrupt leaders as Righteous Judge, in the despair of exile as Suffering Servant. We witness here a high degree of diversity, which led no one to seek to systematize the cult under one timeless image, for the faith was too much in motion to allow for such scholasticism.

Neither biblical writers nor the later rabbis had difficulties with diversity. After all, they took the second commandment seriously, were fully aware that they could not, should not, definitively image God. Yet in their hearts they wanted to focus on the object of their devotion, so they peered *through* the veil into the whirlwind and came up with a rich tapestry of images. Only subsequent Westernization of this rich tradition, plagued with the obsession to decide whether the basic stuff of the universe was fire or water, led to attempts to define God in non-contradictory, propositional terms. We live under that legacy, within a climate where images dare not contradict, for they are supposedly descriptive of a well-defined reality from which the veil of mystery has been lifted. Where dissenting voices are heard, the fear grows that the unity of faith is threatened.

If we look behind scholasticism, however, what do we witness in biblical religion? A climate where anything goes? The bitter polemics against the degrading image of puissant Baal, against the nationalistic gods of the Davidic house and against the Queen of Heaven, prove that not *every* image was tolerated. But what criterion applied? Though Israel's symbols and images were diverse, they do represent a tapestry, not mere shreds and tatters, and the reason is clear: they grow out of a living, developing faith and give expression to a tradition which bore witness to the continuous redemptive creativity of God. Diversity attests to the openness of Israel's perceptivity, and to a remarkable creativity and boldness of spirit in seeking to understand the divine Mystery. Amid diversity, therefore, we can discern in the Bible the unfolding of a profound interpretation of God's relation to creation in terms of guided, purposeful activity. It is only in relation to this central creative, redemptive dynamic that biblical symbols can be understood in their various stages of birth and development. And if the church is to base its self-understanding on the inner dynamic of biblical faith, it will be against the criterion of the dialectical disclosure of divine purpose that symbols and images will be evaluated today.

THE DIVERSITY OF BIBLICAL SYMBOLISM AS MANIFESTATION OF THE FORM/REFORM POLARITY

Now we need to consider more carefully the inner dynamic of biblical faith which traces the disclosure of divine purpose through space and time. As God is not a simple object to be dissected, analyzed, and assigned one name, but the mysterious addressing Subject who transcends human comprehension, likewise the traces of divine word and action in space and time are not simple but rich and diverse. We can preserve the impression of this diversity by observing that the various images which are developed in the Bible cannot be systematized or subsumed under one single image, but interact within the tension-filled form/reform polarity we described earlier, a polarity which is grounded ontologically in two essential aspects of life: *structure* on the one hand and *freedom* on the other, or order and change, or, we might even suggest, law and gospel. It was only amid great struggle and growth that Hebrew religion developed this polarity, and then only imperfectly, for purists wanted it either one way or the other, in antiquity as well as today.

As we have seen, development of the form side of the polarity was already quite advanced before Israelite religion came on the scene. Both the Pharaohs of Egypt and the Lugals of Mesopotamia had constructed a symbolic universe of remarkable order and structure. The healthy society was regarded as an utterly stable society in which kings were kings forever; of course, so were slaves. Thus chaos was controlled by discovery and description of the unchanging structures beneath the flux of visible life. A sacred space was provided by religion within which life could be secure against change and development. Powerful static symbols and images grew out of this system, especially the cosmic temple and the divine king. Not surprisingly the structure of religiopolitical leadership which emanated from this master symbol and divine image was hierarchical, authoritarian, and static, presided over by absolute monarch and hereditary high priest.

The reform side of the polarity was powerfully introduced by Israelite religion, for certain Hebrew slaves were not content with the type of security that bound them with everlasting chains. God the Upholder of an eternal order and Guarantor of the status quo was challenged by God the Liberator. According to this view, the flux of history was not denounced as profane but hailed as the arena of saving divine activity, and thus as the realm of hope for the enslaved and dispossessed. The people of Yahweh entered the world stage as zealous advocates of reform. As a people newly released from slavery, the Israelites accepted only charismatic leaders who proved their divine calling (and utility!) by success in battle. Terms of office were only for the duration of the crisis and were emphatically nonhereditary. It is no accident that women were prominent among those early leaders, for the system was open, dynamic, and forward-moving.

The early laws suggest that a remarkable egalitarian community ideal developed during this early period, but the historiographic sources indicate that the experiment in freedom came to an early and abrupt end, for the young nation found itself on the brink of political chaos. After less than two hundred years of celebrating freedom, a dispirited people went to their charismatic leader and begged for a king that they might be like the other nations, that they might have order and security. Samuel warned them of the kind of authoritarian rule that this would entail, how they would forfeit their freedom. "Never mind, we are weary of defending ourselves, we want not freedom but security, a king, a guarantor of form."

Kings will act like kings, and they did in Israel with a passion. Palaces, fortifications, bureaucracies, and cults were multiplied, and so were taxes. The results were social stratification and curtailment of individual freedom and rights; in a word, oppressive, monolithic form. But the memory of slaves who dared to challenge a mythopoeic orthodoxy of an earlier era engendered a new class of advocates of reform, the prophets. Modeling their office on no authority other than a sense of calling, these critics of rigid, ordered oppression attacked the monolith and kept alive the dynamic concepts of freedom, egalitarian rights, and reform. Their courage to speak out against kings and priests ushered in a creative period in Israel, during which two types of offices coexisted, the one dedicated to order and form, the other dedicated to freedom and reform.

This brief retrospect indicates that symbols and images arose in biblical times within the form/reform polarity. The most creative times were not periods of social equanimity when purists established their ideal and their symbols through the suppression of opposition; the most creative times were characterized rather by the struggles of advocates of form and reform to keep their perspectives alive, to nurture the symbolism and models of leadership which were true to their visions. The long, tension-filled history of biblical symbolism and the tapestry of divine images which it produced are thus the products of a profound view of reality: necessary to life are both the ordering of chaos, which creates space supportive of human existence, and freedom, which encourages the relentless reform of structures which if unrestrained inevitably become instruments of oppression in the hands of the powerful. Within the field of tension demarcated by these twin concerns, a dynamic vision of God's purposes unfolds. This leads to growth in the community of faith's understanding of history and to openness to God's new creative, redemptive acts, a growth and openness also safeguarded by the vision/revision polarity.

BIBLICAL SYMBOLISM AND THE CONTEMPORARY CRISIS IN THE CHURCH

With this brief overview of the function of symbolism in our heritage, let us return to the battle over images and symbols in contemporary church and society. It is not difficult to document changes that have occurred in the last two decades which indicate that a period of glory has passed for the church. The growth and popularity of the Eisenhower era are past for most of the denominations. Crises have arisen in financing programs, recruiting able leadership, and finding ways of relating to an increasingly secular, materialistic society. The perspective of biblical history, however, gives one reason for guarded hope. Spiritual growth is not to be confused with numbers; nor is success, growing out of collusion with a godless system whose arrogant policies the church rubber-stamps, to be equated with the kingdom. The contemporary crisis of faith may be a call back to the theology of the cross, which unmasks triumphalistic displays as a violation of the spirit of a Suffering Messiah. It may be a summons back to an honest evaluation of our forms and structures. After an imperialism reminiscent of Solomon during which prophets were silenced and criticism was deemed unpatriotic in church and society alike, traditional forms may once again be evaluated against the background of the dynamic dimensions of our heritage. The modern crisis may in fact be, on its deepest level, a *krisis,* a period of challenge to decision, allowing the image of the Crucified Messiah to again take a central place in the life of faith. If so, what to the worldly is seen as decline can be interpreted by the spiritual as a challenge to theological vitality and as a sign of God's continued activity on behalf of creation.

If our view of divine purpose were such that we believed that God imposed direction on a passive world, we could content ourselves with the intellectual exercise of observing the interaction of form with reform and vision with revision in an inexorable process of forward movement. If, however, we subscribe to the biblical view of a God who draws humans into divine purpose, the dispassion of the philosophically-minded observer is not enough. The creative balance is a precarious one, into which human response is drawn and has an effect. As heirs of the biblical community of faith we are called upon to become involved in the unfolding of creative, redemptive purpose. Aware that in the area of symbolism the use and abuse of power are at stake, we must ask, "What guidelines can be evolved which encourage a faithful and responsible attitude toward the current struggle over symbols and images?" These guidelines must grow out of the church's commitment to the central dynamic of its faith. For centering on God's ongoing creative, redemptive acts will enable the church to live compassionately and responsibly within the field of tension between form and reform, and to move courageously into a future in which its vision is susceptible to revision as it interacts in worship and service with the living God.

GUIDELINES FOR A
FAITHFUL INTERPRETATION OF SYMBOLS

1. First, we must recognize that the historical-critical study of Scripture does not uncover a single authoritative system of symbols, images, or models of leadership. The reason is simple: symbols and images always are derivative of the world view of a given community. If the world view is a static, mythopoeic one, the symbols will be static. If the world view is a dynamic, historical one, the symbols will evolve with the growth of the tradition. Within the Bible that growth occurs in a lively dialectic between the confessional heritage and new events in-

terpreted as manifestations of divine purpose. Therefore, images and symbols arise out of the dynamics of that dialectic, even as they grow, are replaced, or are impregnated with new meaning. Some are long-lived, some short-lived, but their meaning in any case is determined by how they relate to the inner creative, redemptive dynamic of faith. The problem of symbols and images today cannot be addressed apart from the constant effort of the community of faith to clarify that central dynamic which defines its being and its mission, and which bears it forward. We can go a step further by insisting that a community can be sustained and nurtured by its past only if that central dynamic is incarnated by the community amid the realities and events of this world. The raison d'être of the church is thus one of self-transcending service, which provides the only valid criterion for the evaluation of images, symbols, and leadership models. Preservation on the basis of hoary antiquity alone is idolatry. An image, symbol, or model is justified solely by the service it renders in this incarnational process. To place the test here is not to make discernment a simple process, but it is at least to plug discernment into the proper source.

Now we encounter a powerful resistance to this dynamic view of the function of symbols, images, and models of ministry, a conserving tendency which clothes existing forms in a cloak of immutability. Why is this the case? First, there is a clear basis in social and psychological factors: the vested interests of those in power are best served by a static view of tradition. This derives support from a latent fear among the laity that change will disrupt life and invite chaos. "Really! What will happen when a woman conducts the first mass? What effect will it have on the family, on the young, on the entire social fabric of the land, on the universe!" And we are callous if we do not recognize the deep basis of such fears. After all, the ashes of a fallen structure do not automatically give birth to a fragrant garden.

With patience, therefore, we must address the conservative attitude of our communities vis-à-vis symbols, images, and models of leadership. But patience does not preclude clarity, clarity in pointing out that the slavish adherence to the forms of the past always has and always will lead to institutional petrifaction. We must be clear, moreover, in point-ing out that the ontological basis of the static position is contrary to the inner dynamic of Scripture, for the static position is defensible only on the basis of an ontology which argues that God is no longer active as Creator and Redeemer in our world. Throughout biblical times, God's activity necessitated the growth and development of symbols. To argue for the immutability of existing forms is to subscribe to the "golden age" mentality of myth which Hebrew religion supplanted; it is to betray the rich diversity of our heritage; and above all it is to deny the dynamic movement which our ancestors discerned running through all space and time. To freeze symbolism is to announce that the Kingdom of God has fully arrived, that no groups remain excluded by our present structures, that we need anticipate no further prophets and teachers to challenge and reform. Such a position is uneschatological, unbiblical.

The conservative attitude toward symbols is utterly indefensible if symbols are evaluated from the central dynamic of faith. Such evaluation, moreover, will expose the true motivation behind static entrenchment, which is usually related to control and power.

2. Second, when symbolism, imagery, and models of leadership are subjected to evaluation from the central dynamic of faith, the need to nurture a diversity within the church's symbolism will be recognized. This is necessary first of all since both sides of the form/reform polarity must be addressed, both the need for space secured against chaos and for freedom of growth according to God's creative and redemptive purposes. And in working out models of leadership, room will be provided both for priestly-royal roles and reform-prophetic roles. Correspondingly, the church will be guided by a trustworthy vision with deep roots in a past interpreted as a record of God's faithful providence, but at the same time a radical affirmation of God's ongoing activity will keep alive the revision dimension of a vital confessional community. The strength of the community of faith will not be evaluated, therefore, against the notion of a changeless *pax ecclesiae,* but by an openness to creative polarity which is maintained when a community heeds a divine call to spend itself in self-transcending service in a suffering and complex world.

In an evaluation of symbols, images, and models based on a dynamic notion of the church as the incarnation and manifestation of God's compassion for the world, preferential treatment will be given neither to the old because of its age nor to the new because of its youth. Many old forms will be cherished as exquisite bearers of the creative, redemptive dynamic, for they give a sense of historical depth and are often imbued with the reality which they have borne through the ages. "The Lord is my Shepherd" is a powerful image for many, and "my cup runneth over" a powerful symbol, mainly because of the patina of time and the richness of associations adhering to them. But the contemporary struggle of those experiencing the Liberator of the Oppressed as vividly as did the Hebrews in Egypt can contribute images, symbols, and models that can impregnate old forms with new meaning. We can close our hearts to forms emerging from fresh encounters with the creative, redemptive God only if we adopt an attitude of smug proprietorship over grace, an attitude that will announce to the world the retreat of the church from the liberation struggles involving a God who shows no favorites in the bestowal of grace.

3. Third, the only satisfactory context for the evaluation of symbols, images, and models against the criterion of fidelity to the one true God revealed in acts of creation and redemption is the life of worship, reflection, and self-transcending service of the community of faith. We define such a community as one which is inclusive of all races and classes of humans in all aspects of the decision-making process, that is, where there is no distinction between Jew and Gentile, slave and free, male and female.

4. Finally, a fourth guideline emerges from our past history. In its periods of greatest spiritual vitality and integrity the church has given special emphasis to the reform side of the form/reform polarity and has encouraged the transformation of the very notion of form in fidelity to the eschatological orientation of the vision/revision polarity. Why this has been so in the past is the reason why it must remain so in the present: form, because it so easily can be drawn into the self-serving purposes of the powerful, has as it were a built-in advantage over reform. Everyone is sorely tempted to make God over in one's own image, but those in power are in the favored position to do so. In most religious institutions the image of God the Royal Sustainer of the firm structures which guard against the chaos of unrestrained freedom has an inside advantage over God the Liberator of the oppressed. Therefore, those of us (that is, most of us) whose life style is predicated upon the impoverishment of others must pay heed to a prophetic theology of relinquishment,[5] and this applies not only to possessions but also to positions, not only to satchels but also to symbols.

To acknowledge our need for this fourth guideline is simply to acknowledge our need for prophetic voices in our community today. We have learned from biblical history how those in power were predisposed to ignore the messages of the prophets. Appeal to the need for order and form frequently went hand in hand with attempts to silence the prophets. For the latter spoke out on behalf of those who were denied the benefits of a prosperous society, and their message advocated change.

Let us try to imagine how our society compares with that of ancient Israel during the period of kings and prophets. We are heirs to a society in which religious forces have often added their support to economic and political forces in establishing a privileged elite. Exclusion has fallen along geographic, racial, and sexual lines. Within the church this is recognizable in an authoritative pattern that has characterized most denominations for centuries and only now is beginning to be challenged. It accords special privilege to a white, male, economically privileged group. It claims support on the basis of a mythologized biblicism and a static concept of traditional authority. A particular set of symbols, images, and models of leadership is accepted as authoritative. When this pattern is challenged by excluded elements, the challenge elicits stubborn opposition.

Where are the prophets in this contemporary setting? If we sustain our biblical analogy, it is hard to deny that some are to be found associated with the reform groups who have mustered courage to disturb us with their reinterpretation of biblical symbols and with new symbols born of their own experiences. Thus it is that they hold up before us the Divine Warrior, Mother Earth, Black Brother Jesus, and the Madonna of the Third World. We seek to silence them by an appeal to form: "Images and structures which disrupt order should not be suggested." Here the advantaged position of the custodians of form asserts itself. Though largely derived from our complicity with unjust structures of authority, our defense is couched in an argument intended to sound humane: "Let us not speak of a Divine Warrior; let us expunge this image from our psalms and hymns. We have advanced beyond such bellicose notions of deity and know that God is peace. Mother Earth is crude. Black Jesus is unhistorical. Darkness and night belong to primitive, chthonic deities, and not to our God of light." And thus we, like the kings and princes of Israel, seek to silence the prophetic voices of reform. These voices direct our attention to a God actively engaged *now* in breaking oppressive structures, within the church and without. We tend to ignore any prophetic message which advances a contemporary challenge. We feel more comfortable with a God *once* revealed, with a history which *long ago* was the arena of divine activity, with a selected group of symbols and images which originated in a golden age of the *past* and which are to be applied in support of *our* interests and prejudices. Because of this inherent bias in favor of form, the fourth guideline, urging special emphasis on the reform side of the form/reform polarity, is necessary.

As reform groups reach back into our ancient biblical heritage and there find experiences of divine deliverance resembling their own, they often revive for us symbols and images which we have excluded from our religious consciousness. Often those symbols and images do not accord well with our modern sensibilities. Often they painfully convict us of gross unrighteousness. In our selection of images which comfort, we choose to consign to oblivion images which disturb us.

Let us consider examples of the reinterpretation of symbolism which occurs as the oppressed look at the Bible through the prism of their own experiences. Consider their use, first of all, of the shocking imagery of apocalyptic, imagery which seems so discordant with our modern theological and social views:

Justice is turned back,
    and righteousness stands afar off;
for truth is fallen in the public squares,
    and uprightness cannot enter.
Truth is lacking,
    and he who departs from evil makes himself a prey.

The Lord saw it, and it displeased him
    that there was no justice.
He saw that there was no man,
    and wondered that there was no one to intervene;
then his own arm brought him victory,
    and his righteousness upheld him.
He put on righteousness as a breastplate,
    and a helmet of salvation upon his head;
he put on garments of vengeance for clothing,
    and wrapped himself in fury as a mantle.
According to their deeds, so will he repay,
    wrath to his adversaries, requital to his enemies.
                            (Isa. 59:14–18a)

We find this imagery disturbing, harsh. To ghetto dwellers suffering under the yoke of an exploitative social system, or to guerrillas fighting against severe odds to overthrow a corrupt and unjust government, we commend a "peaceful settlement of differences" and support our recommendation with reference to a God of love.

We close our ears and dismiss their words as rash rhetoric when they draw on the prophets to indict us for a wantonness which has gone so far as to jeopardize the viability of the very earth we inhabit:

> Hear the word of the Lord, O people of Israel;
>> for the Lord has a controversy with the inhabitants of the land.
> There is no faithfulness or kindness,
>> and no knowledge of God in the land;
> there is swearing, lying, killing, stealing, and committing adultery;
>> they break all bounds and murder follows murder.
> Therefore the land mourns,
>> and all who dwell in it languish,
> and also the beasts of the field,
>> and the birds of the air;
>> and even the fish of the sea are taken away.
>
> (Hos. 4:1–3)

To the inhabitants of dilapidated tenements, growing prematurely old for lack of clean air and water and nourishing food, we prefer to speak of the price of scientific progress and to remind them of a God of reconciliation.

We react with indignation when those who have been left out of the benefits of our affluent society describe God in terms derived from their own experiences, that is, as a suffering God who understands the heart of the outcast:

> As many were astonished at him—
>> his appearance was so marred, beyond human semblance,
>> and his form beyond that of the sons of men—
> so shall he startle many nations.
>
> (Isa. 52:14)

To minorities stooped in stature and broken in spirit because of an unjust system from which we reap rich benefits, we prefer to speak simply of a beautiful Savior.

Finally, we hear them describe concentration camps, slums, and starving babies; they plead that we integrate all sides of life into our image of God:

> I form light and create darkness,
>   I make weal and create woe,
>   I am the Lord, who do all these things.
>   (Isa. 45:7)

To those who have experienced life as darkness and day as night we prefer to speak simply of a God of light.

These examples illustrate how richly diverse is the biblical imagery describing God. And openness to this rich diversity is an essential factor in any posture of openness to the will and activity of the living God. Moreover, the temptation to create God in the image of our puny self-image can be resisted only if we supplement our own perception of God's presence with the perception of all of God's children. And the suffering, the poor, and the oppressed play a key role in this respect, for they live at the center of God's redemptive activity in our world today.

All of which is to say that it is impossible to avoid the domestication of our scriptural heritage if our interpretation is carried out in isolation from the needs of the world. We must integrate the experiences of all God's children into our interpretation and appropriation of biblical symbols if we are to avoid using them as idols rather than as windows of transcendence. In her reflections on the first commandment, Brita Stendahl has written: " 'You shall have no other God before me' is an awesome but wonderful commandment, because it forces us to re-examine whether we have got stuck, whether we have old idols instead of a living God."[6] Only if we understand Scripture as the living Word through which God addresses us and summons us to a vision surpassing our own programs, and to purposes transcending our narrow self-interests, can biblical symbols reassert their creative and redemptive power in our communities. For only the living Word is capable of doing the hoeing and winnowing that cultivates and encourages that which gives life and discards that which hinders our being drawn toward the Kingdom of God.

Seen through the experiences of our suffering sisters and brothers, what had become stale and alien images can again become vehicles through which we see more clearly the dynamic creative and redemptive activity of God in our world. For the living God will not be encountered in any symbol which we ensconce as an idol. Rather God is encountered where the poor and the broken struggle to regain their freedom and wholeness. And thus it is that symbols born of such struggles in biblical history find their proper interpretation within the context of analogous struggles occurring in our world today. We must humbly acknowledge our need for the new angle of vision which Blacks, women, and other groups suffering discrimination and oppression can give us on the meaning of the dynamic heart of Scripture. For they can help us clean out our sanctuaries, not of all symbolism, but of symbols which have been turned into idols by being transformed into our own image. And they can help us restore the true meaning and power to many of those same symbols by relating them back to the saving God who is encountered in human lives. Idols, which only draw us deeper into our sinful selves in a vain search for salvation, are thereby replaced by symbols luring us toward the living God, a God who draws us toward our true selves by drawing us toward our sisters and brothers at their points of need.

Once again, in the specific case of biblical symbolism, we are reminded of a truth which applies to all biblical interpretation: we find understanding only if we are grasped by the heart of the living Word; and that occurs within the context where the living Word continues to move in our world, namely, where there are chains, where there is loneliness, where there is hunger, where there is strife. For in such places as these God is active, and there we are called to stand beside our sisters and brothers in their struggles. And in thus relating Word and world, the symbols of Scripture come to life with creative power.

We have thus far indicated that the interpretation of biblical symbolism can be carried on faithfully only as specific symbols are related to the central dynamic of Scripture as that dynamic penetrates the realities of this world. The same applies to the birth of new symbols. We control that process no more than we control God's Spirit. But we must discriminate between faithful and false symbols. And the criterion again is their relation to the central dynamic of our confessional heritage. Where new symbols are born out of the creative and redemptive activity of the God who takes on the cause of the poor, the imprisoned, the oppressed, they give faithful expression to the faith. Where they are invented to enhance the positions of an elite group to the disadvantage of others, they are to be repudiated. In the case of the evaluation of new symbols, as in the case of the interpretation of old symbols, the task is not easy. Only by steadfastly seeking to incarnate the living Word in the world can the church hope to discern and differentiate.

The eschatological openness fostered by the polarities of faith aids the church in its task of interpreting biblical symbols and evaluating new images. It is of course clear that not every symbol will be equally appropriate to every situation. But our basis for choice at least should reach beyond our narrow self-interests to a sense of God's purpose embracing broadly all of creation. This is one of the reasons why even liberation movements, in their intense commitment to redress past injustices, must try to keep alive a perspective reaching beyond their own immediate struggles. For example, such movements must resist the temptation to recast God or Scripture in conformity with their own theology. This is why the *Christian* black militant and the *Christian* feminist are often the object of harsh criticism in those movements. Their devotion lies beyond *any* movement or ideology. Their devotion rests in the one true God, the God of all people.

I shall offer one example of the need to respect the integrity of Scripture, replete as it is with disturbing symbolism, archaic images, and practices that are offensive to modern sensibilities. We have pointed out how it would be wrong for Christians in our country, enjoying peace and prosperity, to expunge from the repertoire of biblical images the image of the Divine Warrior. What is offensive to one group may address another group's experiences powerfully, and the ability of the former to understand the latter is diminished in proportion to its refusal to come to terms with the diverse imagery of the Bible. The specific example to which we refer has to do with principles which guide translators of the Bible. As a member of the Revised Standard Version committee (a committee of the National Council of Churches), I have been involved in the preparation of a new version of the RSV. Among our objectives has been the elimination of masculine-biased language where the masculine bias is absent in the original Greek or Hebrew, having entered in through later translations or the peculiarities of the English language. In a report dated May 9, 1980, and a news release dated June 13, 1980, a special task force on biblical translation of the National Council of the Churches of Christ has urged the RSV committee to "move more boldly."[7] Their motivating rationale is commendable: "This, of all translations, must not lend aid and comfort to sexist attitudes and interpretations." Dr. Edward Powers of the United Church of Christ is quoted as saying, "It is crucial to realize that what we want is a living text, not a museum piece." As for concrete suggestions, the task force urges the RSV committee "to move more boldly" with expressions like "Abraham and Sarah" where the Bible mentions (as bearer of God's promise) only Abraham; "Adam and Eve"; and so forth. "In language about Jesus Christ, we would like to overcome the undesired suggestions that the incarnation makes Christ's maleness crucial in such a way as to overshadow the primary import of the Word having become Flesh, and the Divine having become human." As for language for God, "It is improper to think of God in the analogy of sex and gender."

A serious issue is at stake here. I could not agree more wholeheartedly that the church, if it is true to the living dynamic of its faith, must oppose those who would suggest that God gives special privileges to half of humanity on the basis of gender. But the theological task of the church in making the point clearly and powerfully must be carefully distinguished from the task of translating the Bible. There is no denying the fact that the patriarchal orientation of the Bible and the masculine-biased language it uses for God have added to the oppression of women, especially as the Bible has been used by males to enforce their superiority. But the offensive, inadequate vehicles of expression available to the early Hebrews as they responded to God's activity are a part of an ancient historical record. And the integrity of historical records must be honored. Adding "Sarah" to "Abraham," while a well-intentioned attempt to remove an offense, is a falsification of an historical document. And theologically, it runs contrary to a central tenet of biblical faith: God's revelation has occurred in the real stuff of concrete history and human experience, and it has been handed down to us through confessions using the actual linguistic vehicles of the time, which inevitably reflect the historically conditioned social practices of antiquity. If we rewrite Scripture, we efface the record of God's revelation, which has unfolded over a vast span of time. God's activity has had the dynamic effect of creating a people, a people moving from one level of sensitivity to another. In chapter 2 we saw how the legislation of the eleventh century B.C., according to which only male slaves were to be released in the seventh year, was corrected by the Deuteronomistic school several centuries later to include females. In a myriad of other ways, the masculine bias and the wealth bias and the slave-owner bias have undergone a critique and transformation within Scripture. We must not falsify the long record of that transformation, for it records nothing less than the dynamic creative, redemptive activity of God. And that record is the basis for our discerning a trajectory of redemptive change which reaches to our own time.

The desire to remove the various offenses of the Bible, that is, to rewrite the Bible so as to reflect a contemporary theology, participates in the desire to create a biblical proof text for our own theological position. The Bible has always resisted that, for the Bible cannot provide proof, whether to the slave owner, the liberationist, the socialist, the capitalist, or to anyone else. The Bible addresses all as a living Word which calls them to respond to the living God in faith. This address directs attention to the center of Scripture. That center is delineated not by a process of rational proof but by faithful theological discernment carried out in the church as it engages in interpretation and incarnational living in the world. God's revelation is dynamic. It had a remarkably dynamic beginning in the events of Hebrew slaves. That fact comes through powerfully to us in spite of all time-conditioned vehicles of expression (divine-warrior deity, male bearers of promise, and so forth). But since God's early acts do not end God's creative, redemptive activity, we need not rewrite the description of those acts so as to give expression to the *total* theological confession of the church. We grasp the dynamic historical character of biblical revelation aright only if we study each chapter of the divine-human drama in its *historical particularity* and *confessional specificity*.

We would reformulate Dr. Powers's phrase, quoted above, to read, "What we want is a living *Word*." It is the Word of God, communicated through the various stages of the "text," which is ever-new and dynamic in its unfolding. Last Sunday my ten-year-old daughter Amy sat in church next to me, and I observed as she rewrote the prayers in the bulletin. "God . . . he . . ." was rewritten "God . . . God"; "man" was rewritten "person," and so on. As we came to the prayers in the service, I casually reached for her bulletin and prayed with her, using her "corrected copy." This came very naturally to me. I refrain from referring to God as "he." God transcends gender. As a very personal God, God is equally Mother and Father for me. And so our contemporary prayer was true to our theology, thanks to Amy's editing hand. This audacity came to her, however, not because all masculine-biased language had been removed from the Bible placed in her hands by the church. Rather, the theological education she has received has already taught her that

God did not stop acting when Abraham died. Solomon's Israel does not define our community. Paul's church is not a static model for University Lutheran in Harvard Square. In fact, as far as Amy is concerned, the apostle could soak his head when he admonished women to be silent in the church! The fact that Amy's pastors are a female and a male is an example of the dynamic interpretation she receives of a living Word and a God who continues to act to redeem the oppressed. Of course, we must feel a heavy burden for all the ten-year-old girls who are *not* being taught about a living Word which moves forth from its dynamic biblical matrix to ever-new chapters of expression in the church. But we shall reach those youngsters, and break the shackles authoritarian chauvinists have placed on their tender hearts, not by "whitewashing" Scripture but by providing religious instruction imbued with the creative, redemptive dynamism which moves through the heart of our biblical-confessional heritage.

All of us, young and old, will have both the courage and the grace to make room for the living God in our lives only if we feel drawn into God's purpose, which transcends our personal fears and needs. For then we shall participate as Christ's body in the interpretation and transformation of symbolism in a manner true to our mission of reconciliation on behalf of God's *entire* family. We shall not drive out of our community the prophetess who tears the cloak from a patriarchal idol which in the past has given some of us a privileged birthright. We shall instead beg for forgiveness and learn from her concerning God's new acts of redemption. We shall break ourselves free from the hypnotic gaze and warmth of the Aryan Jesus of blond curls and blue eyes, and dare to look into the determined eyes of a Jewish end-time preacher. We shall repudiate the cozy covenant between Western capitalists and a developer deity, and address seriously the effects of a broken covenant. With those who have struggled and lost we shall have the courage to look at the darkness behind the silver lining of our facile theologies. Courage to be addressed by the living God amid a rich diversity of ancient and modern symbols can be derived only from a groundedness of our identity in the exclusive lordship of the one true God. Those who hold to other devotions will undoubtedly continue to make appeal to the mythopoeic God of form and call this fidelity to Scripture, whereas the proper word for such an appeal is bibliolatry.

As modern Christians we do well to consider our options soberly.

We can clutch selfishly at our idols and our biased interpretations, and die spiritually amid dead symbols and images as have devotees of many other cults. Or we can learn the gracious art of relinquishment, an art possible only to those who are related to the living God, only to those who are not their own, not dedicated to defending themselves and their pet symbols. It is an art possible only to those who feel drawn into a purpose which transcends self and includes all God's creation. Then we can be children of God, reappropriating biblical symbols infused with new meaning, and enriching our vocabulary for God, world, and each other by learning from those engulfed in liberation struggles today fresh new ways of addressing life and God. To do so involves dying, to be sure, not dying of the church but dying of sinful selves. Through such dying comes the discovery of life drawn into a creative, redemptive current which runs through all reality, and which guides reality toward its intended goal of peace wedded with justice.

The guidelines and illustrative examples we have given are not intended to be definitive or even systematic. They only point out some of the implications which flow from the effort to place the controversy over sounding gongs and clashing symbols within a historical and theological framework that allows us to transcend the pettiness which usually characterizes such debate. Furthermore, they illustrate how awareness of inner-biblical polarities can direct our attention beyond the surface meanings (and discords) of symbols and images to the inner dynamic which they, often in their interaction, convey through the ages. We are heirs to a heritage which does not uphold consistency and homogeneity as the foremost tests of faith, but fidelity to the one true living God. Our God is not dissectible object but ineffable addressing Mystery, and faithful response to God implies richness, diversity, openness and honesty with one another. As a mere beginning, that richness embraces God the Father *and* God the Mother, the Creator of light *and* darkness, King *and* Liberator, *deus absconditus* and *deus revelatus*. As we reach out to broaden our understanding of old symbols and to enrich our vocabularies with the new symbols and images of sisters and brothers coming from different experiences, we step into life from grace rather than from proprietorship and find ourselves embraced by the divine Mystery as one human family. Within that family we find communion with the Ineffable One toward whom our diverse symbols reach and from whom alone they and we derive meaning and purpose.

CHAPTER 6

The Faithful Response (2)

Action Which

Incarnates the Living Word

THE NATURE OF AUTHORITY IN A
DYNAMIC VIEW OF SCRIPTURE

Modern hermeneutical theories have drawn attention to the central importance of language, both in everyday life and in our understanding the classics of the past. Through language reality addresses us, challenges us to understand our nature and purpose in life more deeply, and points us in the direction of heightened sensitivity to and perceptivity of the world around and within us. Application of these insights to biblical interpretation can contribute to our understanding of the language of Scripture in ways which transform the perplexing questions raised for faith by modernity into exciting opportunities for growth. And indeed, such insights, when applied to Scripture, expose levels of significance beyond those discovered in other writings. For through the words of the Bible we confess that we are addressed not only by the views of past generations, and not merely by an abstract concept of reality, but by Reality revealed to us over a long, continuous history in intimate, personal terms as Yahweh, Spirit, and Father of Jesus Christ.

The personal form of address which the church encounters in the Bible leads now from the response in words, discussed in the preceding chapter, to the question of the faithful response in action. As background to this question, however, we need to clarify further how it is that the Bible serves as a vehicle of God's Word in defining what responses are actually faithful ones. What we do not want to suggest is that in every situation a biblical injunction can be found which prescribes exactly what action is demanded by God. The Bible is not a recipe book. Nor is it a prison cell delimiting the arena of God's words and acts. The God who addresses every generation anew defies confinement in the cult of bibliolatry. Moreover, any attempt to set limits on the sovereign God contradicts the central dynamic of Scripture itself. Does this assertion, however, not simply deny that the Bible has a unique status? Is not the universal Word then to be found in every profound exploration of reality? Why the disproportionate amount of attention paid to the Bible by Christians addressing the questions of life when whole libraries stand open for their perusal?

One straightforward answer to these questions appeals to the status of the Bible as canon of the Christian church. This answer is helpful *if* understood historically, that is, if canonization is evaluated as an important point in the development of the confessional heritage. But canonization threatens to replace a dynamic understanding of the living Word of God with a static myth if it is understood ahistorically as a divine seal signifying that within the pages of Scripture the total revelation of divine will is found in immutable propositional form. Like all other symbols, doctrines, creeds, and council decisions, the canon should be understood as an expression of the unfolding, dynamic movement of our confessional heritage.

Because the Word of God coming to expression in the Bible, and the saving acts to which the biblical narratives bear witness, are not whimsical outbursts or disjointed episodes but stages in one divine drama, they are unified around a common center and manifest a dynamic trajectory. Discernment of that center and that trajectory by the community of faith led to the various efforts at defining a canon, which in historical terms are to be seen as efforts at self-definition by God's people. Early Christians were in effect saying, Here are the writings which constitute the paradigms of our faith. And we benefit greatly from those attempts, for the same task is very much with us today as well. In our task, however, we must not substitute their struggle to relate to the dynamic heart of their heritage for our responsibility to do the same. For abdication of our responsibility would come at the cost of a weakening of our contact with God's living Word, a Word defined not by endpapers but by an address from the heart of Scripture which encounters every generation anew.

Here an example is pertinent. Martin Luther, like saints of many ages, did not blindly accept all books of the Western canon as equally authoritative in any formalistic manner. As one addressed by the living Word speaking out from the dynamic center of Scripture, Luther responded by identifying the heart of the Bible, that is, by describing the gospel of Jesus Christ as a canon within a canon. This identification grew out of his location of the center of Scripture in Christ and was expressed thus: *Was Christum treibet* ("What drives one to Christ").

If the church is conscious of being addressed by the living Word, it will once again clearly conceptualize the role of the Bible in dynamic terms. It will not engage in "question begging" by pulling the formal category of canon out of a hat but will discern in the Bible the foundational confessions and events which set the trajectory of the creative, redemptive movement that bears all reality toward God's kingdom of peace wedded with justice. In the Christ event that kingdom was revealed to the community of faith with an intensity which gives the dynamic trajectory of our confessional heritage a center. And since the church today lives under the lordship of that same Messiah, its connection with its biblical heritage is not only unbroken but personal.

Here we shall briefly summarize what we believe to be the essential characteristics of a dynamic view of Scripture. In so doing we seek to express the unique role of Scripture in our understanding of revelation without placing spatial or temporal limits on God's sovereignty.

1. Amid the particularities of the social, political, and historical realities of biblical times, and through the linguistic vehicles with which ancient believers responded to God's initiative, God was revealing a purpose which pertains to all times and to all peoples. In the incarnation of Jesus Christ that purpose is revealed more clearly and personally than in any other event.

2. God's revelation has continued in a manner consistent with the creative, redemptive trajectory set forth in the foundational events and confessions of the Bible; hence, an unbroken chain of testimony links us with those ancient writings in the form of our confessional heritage.

3. The context within which God's revealed purpose has been related to contemporary realities (themselves viewed as manifestations of God's ongoing activity) has always been the community of faith, and so it is today as well.

4. Membership in the community of faith implies assent to the fact that the confessional heritage, while replete with the blemishes of human limitation and imperfection, is nonetheless a *faithful* witness to God's

purpose, even as the community which carries that heritage forth, while equally imperfect, is the context within which God's grace enters the lives of repentant sinners and draws them together into a communion of self-transcending service.

Though we believe the above four points grow out of the central dynamic of Scripture itself, they are obviously presuppositional in nature. It is therefore proper to consider two objections that will arise in the minds of many Christians.

Objection 1. A dynamic view of revelation is an invitation to subjectivism. The only way to safeguard revelation against such subjectivism is to accept the words of Scripture as propositional truth, inerrant and infallible.

Reply. This objection fails to acknowledge that it has merely replaced one presupposition with another, one just as susceptible to the mistaken subjective judgment of the human interpreter as the other. That the nature of revelation in Scripture is in the form of inerrant, infallible propositions is an enormous presupposition. It can be criticized best from what is admittedly a conclusion drawn from critical theological reflection, namely, that the propositional posture runs counter to the essential inner dynamic of scriptural faith. According to this dynamic, God has guided, and continues to guide, the community of faith in understanding its essential being as God's servant people. Since discernment of the direction of that growth in understanding is not any individual's brainchild but the product of the community's growth in the midst of worship and service, it is not lacking in safeguards against hazardous subjectivity.

Objection 2. The dynamic view of Scripture represents an erosion of biblical authority.

Reply. We do not merely pick or choose at will what episode or aspect of our confessional heritage we wish to advance in defense of a given decision. Rather that heritage, in its stories, confessions, symbols, and images, reveals a plan for reality. We make decisions in the light of that plan and with the conviction that we participate in God's purposes through our decisions and acts. Within that heritage there has also developed an understanding of what it is to be God's people. This has generated guidelines, laws, and a vivid style of being, which tutor us in living within a covenant with the one true God.[1] These guidelines, as they evolve and are criticized and refined within the context of the whole people, are not just up for grabs in each new generation. Thus there is both an understanding of divine purpose and an understanding of what it is to be God's people, which come to us with three thousand years of background. And the fact that the understandings are concretely embodied in a community we embrace as our own means that we take them with utmost seriousness in our daily decisions. One can therefore try to argue that the dynamic view of Scripture provides no authoritative basis for decisions in faith and living, but only if one has a very sterile concept of authority, faith, and living. If our concept is as much alive as the living God to whom we are drawn, we receive from our confessional heritage a very distinct way of responding to grace and of discerning where God is at work "to make and keep human life human in the world."[2]

So often the mandate of how to be faithfully human comes to us from this heritage in such utter clarity that the only danger lies in our cunning efforts to dodge it for love of sin.

> [God] has showed you, O man, what is good;
>   and what does the Lord require of you
> but to do justice, and to love kindness,
>   and to walk humbly with your God!
>   (Mic. 6:8)

We are not lacking an authoritative basis for decision in the church today. What we *are* lacking is the clear sense of our not being our own, of our being Christ's body, which sense alone can overcome our complicity in worldly schemes, a complicity that prevents our taking a stand for justice because we are so much a part of that which God calls us to oppose. We cannot love God and mammon, God and personal power, God and special privilege. We as a church and as individuals either give ourselves to God's kingdom completely, or we open ourselves to the authority of whatever gods we actually serve.

A dynamic view of Scripture therefore does not erode authority. It makes it immediate and intensely personal. For from the event located at the center of the trajectory of our confessional heritage comes a renewal of our relationship to God which replaces legalistic authority with commitment to the living God and God's Messiah. The Apostle Paul experienced God's new gift in Jesus Christ as qualitatively so new that he could describe it as a new creation (2 Cor. 5:17; Gal. 6:15). This term is rich in connotations, implying both the ongoing character of God's involvement with the human family and the indivisibility of the creative and redemptive sides of God's activity. Adumbrated in the life of communion with God which the disciples shared with Christ was the fellowship intended by God from the dawn of human civilization. The long-awaited kingdom wedding universal justice and peace had been inaugurated by God's Messiah. A people separated from God had experienced reconciliation. As heirs to this new creative, redemptive act, we are to live as a new humanity, and that means as a people experiencing divine authority as an internal summons to be true to our nature as the body of Christ, a condition not to be confused with obedience imposed by a code of law. To substitute a static, external authority for this dynamic authority of the new covenant would be to turn back the hands on God's creative, redemptive timetable. It would amount to the repudiation of God's grace, and a betrayal of a relationship which is new every day.

Thus those who claim that a dynamic view of Scripture destroys authority have confused the authority derived from the total experience of dedication to the living God with authority confined to written formulations. We are recipients of a history of divine grace, which has drawn us into communion with one another and into service of all our brothers and sisters, and thereby we are participants in the inbreaking of God's kingdom. The basis of our authority in deliberating on how the church and individuals are to act in a given setting is thus the same one which in chapter 5 we identified and applied in the task of evaluating symbols and images. It is derived from the central dynamic of our confessional heritage and from our experience of being drawn by our Creator, Redeemer, Sustainer, and Judge into that dynamic as agents of peace, justice, and reconciliation in the world, which is to say, as the body of Christ in the world.

We have now differentiated two ways of viewing the relationship between the Bible and the faithful response in action. We deem inadequate a view of the Bible as a formal authority consisting of truths and laws delivered to another age which we are obliged to observe, or as a collection of stories of a golden age of revelation which we are required to reenact. We believe rather that the Bible portrays a creative, redemptive dynamic which moves at the center of all reality and guides creation toward God's goal of a kingdom wedding peace with justice. Moreover, we believe that such a portrayal is accompanied by the Word of the living God which addresses us as church and individuals and calls us into active participation in that redemptive drama.

FOUR QUALITIES OF THE
FAITHFUL RESPONSE IN ACTION

This dynamic view of Scripture now permits us to pose the question of how the church and its individual members determine the faithful response in action, for such action will be seen as growing out of the church's role as partner in God's ongoing creative, redemptive plan for creation. We shall identify certain qualities of the faithful response in action.

1. The source of the first quality of the faithful response is an overwhelming sense of gratitude to God. The creative, redemptive drama which we see unfolding, the Word which we hear calling us to participate in that drama, and the evidence of divine providence on all sides of us and within us thoroughly condition the response of God's people. Our lives are founded upon grace. The initiative in the drama to which we are called is God's initiative alone. This confers a distinct quality on the faithful response in action, that of gentle trust and humility. We are not proprietors of grace but recipients, for we are drawn not into our own purposes but into the self-transcending purposes of God. Arrogance and self-aggrandizement are excluded from a movement dedicated to a vision of peace and justice intended for all people. Rather, gratitude creates a yearning to be drawn into the stream which flows at the heart of life and spends its healing waters on all God's creation.

2. As a second quality of the faithful response in action we recognize commitment to the one true God. Even as the meaning of Scripture is understood by grasping the heart of the biblical message, so too the faithful response arises within the heart of the believing community and individual. For without the purity and proper orientation of the heart, faithfulness is impossible. Kierkegaard formulated this well: "Purity of heart is to will one thing." Christians are centered individuals, for they acknowledge only one God, and that is the living God whom they have come to know and love through being addressed by the Word and

by being drawn into the redemptive drama portrayed in the confessional heritage. When we describe the faithful response in action, therefore, we speak of commitment, for only commitment to the living God will purify motives and open our minds to a purpose which transcends our own selfish desires. The quality of purity of heart to will one thing gives proper accent to the existential moment in faith. We are related in our scripturally based faith to the living God who addresses us now. Our time, like that of every generation of the faithful before us, is a *krisis*, a time of decision, for God's plan is at the very center of the events which surround us. In being drawn into the quality of action mandated by the living Word, we are being drawn toward the living God.

3. Gratitude and commitment create the proper conditions for the faithful response in action, and they create not a passive attitude but one which focuses the attention of the community of faith on the next quality of the faithful response in action, namely, discernment of God's purpose as it has been revealed in our confessional heritage. The idea of community involvement in God's creative, redemptive drama excludes subjective sentimentalism. Responding to grace and centering on the one true God in total commitment mandate an important task, namely, discernment and careful conceptualization of the divine plan which has unfolded over the course of our confessional history. Only with reverence and humility does the community of faith engage in this task, for it is mindful both of the veil which separates humans from the mind of God and of the blemished nature of the church's response to divine initiative over the ages. Nevertheless, the task is accepted as a responsibility growing out of our confession that God is one and that God's acts over the expanse of time and space are expressive of a unified purpose. Moreover, *where* we look in the effort to conceptualize the purposeful stream running at the center of history and cosmos is answered by the biblical view of God as a God whose purposes have come to light in the concrete happenings of history and in the experiences of a particular people. Within Scripture we therefore can discern the unfolding of a creative, redemptive plan which finally embraces all peoples.

What we are here calling the discernment and conceptualization of God's plan revealed in Scripture, and what we have elsewhere called the envisioning of Dynamic Transcendence, is one of the most important tasks of the church today. It amounts to nothing less than portraying the dynamic heart of the Word of God by which the church is addressed, and describing the living stream which flows through the confessional heritage. In other words, it encompasses biblical theology, history of dogma, systematic theology, and ethics. It is a task, moreover, which is not in any way restricted to theological faculties. It is carried out in task forces of the church, in the life of every parish, and in the decisions of the individual believer. Naturally such conceptualization, which calls for the deepest insight and the highest creativity the church can marshal, cannot be accomplished here. We can, however, describe two facets of the task.

One facet is the description of the agelong trajectory which extends through the Bible and the history of the church. This is best done with the use of images, and perhaps the most powerful image is the archaic one of the Kingdom of God. Over the course of God's dealing with the community of faith, a Kingdom has unfolded. It has unfolded in the field of tension between an ideal and reality, a field replete with the stress and struggle of the form/reform and the visionary/pragmatic polarities. It is a kingdom that has resisted all attempts of kings and priests to circumscribe it, for it is not definable by human boundaries. Ultimately it is the reign of no human, but of God, and its territory is no one nation but the hearts of all who love the God of righteousness. The unfolding of this kingdom, however, is related intimately to a specific history, that of the Jewish people. It developed under David, Hezekiah, Josiah, and in the figure of the suffering servant. Finally, and most remarkably, it developed in the life of Jesus Christ. Beyond the chapters of biblical history, moreover, it has continued to unfold, sometimes visibly in key persons or events, more often as a leaven in the world, silently working for reconciliation, peace, and justice among all humans. Certainly use of the image of the kingdom is not the only means possible for tracing this trajectory, but it serves as an illustration of the fact that the dynamic reality at the center of our confessional heritage can be described. That is to say, the task of discerning and carefully conceptualizing the divine plan revealed in Scripture challenges the church to apply the best of its talent and creativity in order that it may bear witness to the living stream which it believes has guided reality from the very beginning.

The second facet in the task of discerning and conceptualizing God's plan is the description of the paradigms of faith. These are events which reveal the nature of God's plan with special clarity. Taken together, they document in the specifics of life God's relationship with God's people. Though each paradigmatic event is seen as a new manifestation of God's plan, a unity of purpose is discernible through them all, a fact underlying the phenomenon of typological exegesis, which has been popular throughout our confessional history, from the biblical writers themselves down to modern exegetes like Karl Barth and Gerhard von Rad. For example, in the Exodus event the Jews recognized God's purpose with a poignancy which still serves as Judaism's clearest window on transcendence. In the return from Babylonian captivity they discerned the unfolding of God's plan in a second exodus, more glorious than the former but consistent with its basic trajectory. The redemption celebrated in the Christ event and symbolized in the Eucharist takes up the theme of the earlier paradigms in a new expression of God's plan that draws Christians toward the kingdom which God has intended for all humans from the beginning of the covenant relationship. Thus, as the church goes about the task of discerning and conceptualizing God's plan for creation, the paradigms of faith add richness to the trajectory of divine purpose by infusing specific content and an immediacy which relates readily to our own experiences.

4. The fourth quality of the faithful response in action, namely, its being guided by a vision of divine purpose, rests on the third. For the discernment and conceptualization of the divine plan running through history comes to life in the church as a contemporary reality by describing for the faithful the ultimate direction and meaning of life. The creative, redemptive stream continues to bear reality toward the goal intended by God. And that stream, or trajectory, or kingdom, or manifestation of Dynamic Transcendence (to use, but not to exhaust, possible metaphors), constitutes the vision which defines for us the nature of reality and our mission in it. From the purposeful movement which we are able to discern there comes our sense of identity and purpose, and from this sense we can determine the faithful response in action.

In incorporating these four qualities of the faithful response in action, the church is living true to its identity as an extension of the biblical community of faith. The biblical community of faith was the gathering of the faithful in worship and service before the *mysterium tremendum*. It was drawn into God's purpose by being the matrix within which contemporary happenings and realities were interpreted as manifestations of God's ongoing activity. This interpretation of reality, which perceived beneath surface manifestations a divine plan for the world, arose from the perspective furnished by the confessional heritage. Where that perspective revealed the struggle for righteousness taking place, the community of faith recognized a familiar pattern, the pattern of God's activity. And to that place the community of faith was drawn to respond in action by taking sides with those suffering for the sake of righteousness.

The church today carries forward the history of the community of faith. Thus is carried forward, too, the commission to participate in God's activity by interpreting contemporary happenings and realities from the perspective of its confessional heritage, by discerning where God is active in the world, and by dedicating its total energy to God's creative, redemptive plan and the goal of universal reconciliation and healing. To be sure, this involves a very sensitive and exacting process of interpretation and discernment, for the confessional heritage which bears witness to God's purpose is rich in diversity, even as the realities to which we are to apply our vision are complex. And the church will not live out its commission responsibly if it reduces its rich heritage to conform to existing programs or ideologies. The only adequate safeguard against such reductionism is constant, faithful study of the biblical and confessional heritage, so as to enable the Word of God to address the church in uncompromised intensity and integrity. Since the polarities of faith discussed in chapters 2, 3, and 4 help preserve the dynamic addressing nature of Scripture, we now ask how they contribute to the faithful response in action.

THE VISIONARY/PRAGMATIC POLARITY AND THE FAITHFUL RESPONSE IN ACTION

We look first at the visionary/pragmatic polarity. Through the task of discerning and conceptualizing God's plan for creation, described above as the third quality of the faithful response in action, a vision is derived. It is a vision of the direction in which reality, under God's guidance, is being drawn, and of the obstacles inhibiting free movement toward that goal. From this vision is derived our identity as church and as individual Christians. That is to say, in the light of this vision, with its picture of a transcendent meaning and direction in life, we, to use the Apostle Paul's phrase, no longer regard one another "from a human point of view" (2 Cor. 5:16). Our being is grounded in God. Our meaning is determined by God's purpose. As church, we have a new name which is descriptive of this new being, "the body of

Christ," and as individual Christians we have a new name equally descriptive of our being, "new creation." With our corporate and individual life grounded in divine grace, we are no longer threatened in any ultimate sense by earthly powers.

The vision/translation, or visionary/pragmatic, polarity has more to say about this identity: it is eschatological through and through. What we are as a new creation we do not hold as a personal possession, and as body of Christ we do not control our destiny. We grow into this new reality as we are drawn toward God's purpose for creation. That purpose is unfolding in the world, that is to say, in an order which is not aware of the new creation God intends it to be. This task of being ambassadors of Christ in a world which does not recognize its Redeemer brings with it the dialectic of faith.

Within the dialectic of faith we bear the responsibility of integrating our vision into the pragmatic realities of a fallen order. That is to say, ours is the prophetic task of translation and integration. And unless our personal or communal world collapses into a chaos which obliterates all sense of order and banishes all hope for reform, that is to say, unless we face the persecution and oppression of Daniel or John of Patmos, apocalyptic escape into the vision represents abdication of our responsibility. It is important that the church and the individuals who accept the responsibility of translating the vision be aware of the tension within which they will live. They must remind pure pragmatists, as did Isaiah, that human possibilities provide an insufficient basis for responsible decisions. And they must remind pure visionaries that religious experiences which refuse to relate to a tainted world are escapist, not prophetic.

The tension goes even further. It is internal within the church and the individual as well. As the church evaluates its mission, it must confess that it lives within a state of now/not yet: *now* it is participating in the Kingdom of God, *now* it embodies the body of Christ; but *not yet* does it fulfill its role in faithfulness. The visionary/pragmatic tension can allow the church to live with the ambivalence, for the tension reminds the church that its identity as body of Christ *is* genuine, even though that genuineness is eschatological. Luther's visible/invisible church polarity describes this same dialectic. The tension it implies is felt as well when we describe the church as an agent of divine activity, or as the matrix within which contemporary events are viewed through the lens of the confessional heritage to discern where God is active.

While such descriptions do point to the role of the church, we are ever mindful of the tension between the now and the not yet.

Similarly, the individual confesses to a now/not yet. *Now* his or her essential nature is understood in terms of the new creation, and this identity grounds faith and confidence firmly on God's grace. Nevertheless, as moments of doubt and acts of faithlessness continue to remind us, we still yearn for the *not yet*. And daily we repent and pray to be drawn more completely into God's plan. *Simul justus et peccator!* We derive our identity from the vision. But we live as translators of that vision in a fallen world, a world that remains ingrained in us as the "old Adam."

The tension implied by the visionary/pragmatic polarity is not an easy one, but it reminds us of our essential task as servants given to a purpose transcending ourselves. We pray every day that we may become what we are in Christ, a new creation. And we pray that the world may become what it is intended by God to be, a kingdom wedding universal peace and justice. The faithful response in action thus issues forth from our understanding of the vision and the translation for which it is intended. As church and as believers we are to do whatever is required to translate the vision of the kingdom of God into the realities of this world. The most perfect expression of this is found in the bread, the water, the clothes, and the kindness given "to one of the least of these my brethren," and thus "to me" (Matt. 25:31–46). Where a local parish takes a stand against racism, where the church at large campaigns against world hunger, where an individual believer befriends an alcoholic or stands beside one bereaved of a loved one, the kingdom is at hand. We shall develop later a concrete example of the faithful response in action. Here we seek to glimpse the overall picture of our vision: God intends that all reality be drawn into the kingdom, for "in Christ God was reconciling the world to himself," and from that vision of God's purpose and God's activity is derived our response in action: ". . . and entrusting to us the message of reconciliation" (2 Cor. 5:19).

The biblical visionary/pragmatic polarity thus locates the arena of the faithful response in action in the midst of this world. But the church does not go about frantically applying this program and then that; rather it steadfastly seeks to understand the world and respond to its events from the perspective of its transcendent vision.

To this we wish to add another implication of the visionary/pragmatic polarity. It grows out of another characterization we have used for this polarity, namely, vision/revision. Even as we observed how in the Bible the translation of the vision into the ongoing realities of this world implied an accompanying revision, even so will the church appreciate the dynamic, unfolding nature of its vision today. In the Bible the phenomenon of revision was predicated on the understanding of God as a living God, active in every generation anew. And we confess that the living God is active in our world as well. Hence, in our efforts faithfully to translate the vision into the realities of this world, we are aware of participating in God's ongoing work. It follows that anyone who thus lives in the presence of God must be open to new lessons from history and experience. The vision of the church, therefore, will continue to undergo revision as God's purposes continue to unfold. Of course, this implies openness within the church to different versions of the vision. It also emphasizes how much the church has to learn from those on the frontiers of human struggle today—Blacks, Latin Americans, women, the poor. Revision does not imply, however, a casting about for novel remedies, or careless about-faces, for the actions of the church are on the cutting edge of a millenniums-long trajectory of divine activity. God's act in our day is new, but at the same time it is true to a very long, steadfast history of creation and redemption. Therefore, the church's activity will be open to the new, even as it remains true to the agelong purpose of universal reconciliation revealed within its confessional heritage.

The visionary/pragmatic polarity thereby engenders in the church a fitting posture for acting as agent of the divine purposer. It comes with a distinct word for a foundering world, for its careful discernment and conceptualization of God's plan in the past equips it with a vision of what God is purposing today. But at the same time, the eschatological character of its vision guards against the abuse of the vision for debased purposes. The church remains open to new lessons, it remains sensitive to the visions of others, it seeks to discern the activity of God wherever God is active. It sets no limits, it shuns proprietorship. Within the field of tension preserved by this polarity, then, the church is able to live graciously with its in-process character. Eschatological openness in no way detracts from its resolve to respond faithfully in action, for it is sent to a world for which God has expressed the depths of divine compassion in the ultimate gift of God's Son.

We may note that the vision/revision polarity also helps the church to maintain a healthy posture vis-à-vis the other religions of the world.

It avoids arrogance and insensitivity on the one hand, indecisiveness and false modesty on the other. Its openness to the visions of other faiths is assured both by the eschatological perspective of its vision and by the universal scope of its understanding of God's purpose. At the same time, its own identity confidently and graciously rests on a careful conceptualization of God's plan as manifested in its long confessional history.

THE FORM/REFORM POLARITY AND THE FAITHFUL RESPONSE IN ACTION

Having noticed how the visionary/pragmatic polarity aids the church in its search for the faithful response in action, we turn now to examine the contribution of the other polarity we discussed. In the Old Testament, we observed how transmitters and editors refused to resolve the tension between form and reform. Royal psalms celebrating the eternal dynasty and the abiding order it preserves are found alongside prophetic diatribes against every alliance between structures of governance and oppression of the weak. We even noticed how prophets themselves strove to maintain the form/reform polarity; how, for example, Samuel (if we may consider him a "proto-prophet") presupposed the stability of the forms he sought to reform, how Hosea condemned the excessive reform zeal of Jehu because it led to social chaos, and how Isaiah infused the royal Davidic ideal with the reform dynamic of the League and the prophets.

As heir to this second polarity, the church searches for the faithful response in action with sensitivity to the human need for form and reform. Judiciousness is called for, therefore, in addressing those complex issues in life which so often elicit the "pure" solutions of kings or of zealots. Life is not viable in chaos, and hence order and form are necessary. But the church must consistently be on guard against the tendency for it to be co-opted by powerful representatives of structured self-interest. This occurs so easily because the church's institutional needs often coincide with the needs of other institutions in the society. The reform side of the polarity, without which the church simply blends into the institutional landscape of the country, can be preserved only if the church's self-definition arises from its identity as an extension of the biblical community of faith. Its mission is to embody the dynamic vision of the kingdom, a kingdom which grows within the form/reform polarity.

There is also a personal dimension to the form/reform polarity, one that lies at the center of our experience of reconciliation. In the new creation which we have become by God's grace, we observe the stability of a form dimension, for as a creation of God, born of divine grace, our lives are placed on a dependable foundation. In the biblical narrative, the waters divided at the command of God, and a land opened up to wandering slaves to establish a space for God's people. Laws and ordinances and social practices evolved to preserve and enhance this space or form. Water has become a type for the space which God has created for us, for baptism is a manifestation of form. We are the new creation because of a gift of grace. We can depend on a foundation upon which to construct our lives as individuals and as a community. Death, the devil, principalities, and powers cannot destroy that foundation. When they tried, their dominion was broken by *Christus Victor*. "Built on a Rock the Church Doth Stand." When we seem about to collapse, we cling to the cross, feel the reality of our baptism, and confess that there is a foundation to life; life, by grace, has form.

We go on immediately—as did Paul when he moved from the first eleven chapters of Romans to chapters 12–16—from the gift to the response. Form and a sure foundation are given to us as a platform from which to respond in the reform activities that are a part of our vision. From the earliest stages of biblical faith, the Covenant, while predicated on God's prevenient acts of gracious deliverance, drew the people into solemn commitment to obey the commandments inferred from God's acts in history. In the New Covenant, the tie between God's initiative and our response in obedience has become even more intimate, being etched upon our hearts. Therefore, the assurance we have of a form in life and the gift of space to be God's new creation are not taken for granted or abused but gratefully accepted as the form and space within which we engage in a life of self-transcending service. As servants and as a servant church, we are drawn into God's program of reforming and renewing a fallen world, a world intended for peace and justice.

THE CHURCH AS BODY OF CHRIST

By way of summarizing the points we have been making about the faithful response in action, we turn to a closer analysis of the metaphor of the church as Body of Christ.[3] It draws together the inner dynamic of the biblical trajectory and the paradigms of faith into one powerful image. We have observed how the church can respond faithfully to God's grace by being drawn into the drama of creation and reconciliation as a willing participant. It does so as it accurately envisions the unfolding of the kingdom of God and translates the qualities of that kingdom into the structures and realities of this world. From its master paradigm of the life of Christ it learns that that translation occurs when the vision, or the Word of God, becomes incarnate in the world. Therefore, the church models its life after the life of Christ, that is to say, it understands itself as the body of Christ in the world even as it understands its commission as that of incarnating the Word, or the inner dynamic of its confessional heritage, in the world. We can characterize this incarnational process by describing the body of Christ in terms of its heart, mind, and members.

1. First, for the church to have the heart of Christ is for it to embody a compassion which embraces the feelings of all hearts, of all people in the world. The broken heart of a Sahara mother unable to find food for her starving baby, the confused heart of the teenage alcoholic, the angry heart of the youthful militant, the yearning heart of the political exile, these are all embraced by the church which embodies the heart of Christ. Wherever a church becomes a gathering of a select few out of the world, feelings narrow and a pitiable, shriveled heart replaces the heart of Christ. Indeed the narrowing of vision usually does not stop until the circle narrows to embrace only the alienated individual, cut off from other humans, and viewing faith and all other aspects of life solely in terms of what he or she can get out of them for self. The shriveled heart becomes a heart of stone. Not so should it be in the body of Christ, which moves in ever broader circles until it has found ways in which the entire human family can be embraced by the love of God.

2. Second, the church is to have the mind of Christ. The heart of Christ relates to the gratitude and commitment which we earlier described as the first two aspects of the faithful response in action. The mind of Christ in turn relates to the latter two aspects of conceptualizing the plan of God manifested in our confessional heritage and of deriving from that plan a vision of the church's role and mission today. The church which faithfully embodies the mind of Christ will make decisions and take actions that respect the needs, longings, and rights of all people. Its efforts will be dedicated to the reconciliation of the members of the entire human family with one another and with God. If the

church, in its theological endeavors, its proclamation, and its social outreach, embodies the mind of Christ, it will break a common pattern of self-service on behalf of the favored and the powerful within the church. The mind of Christ offers a self-transcending perspective from which to make decisions and to take actions. It alone can assure that the response in action will be faithful, that is, dedicated to God's kingdom of peace and justice.

3. Finally, the church is the body of Christ in its many diverse members, each with his or her individual gift to offer. This aspect of the body metaphor which the Apostle Paul developed (1 Corinthians 12) is especially pertinent today, for translation of the vision involves complexities confounding the mind of any single individual. Called for is the expertise of many different disciplines if the church is to offer responsible and credible counsel from the perspective of its vision. We have also observed how exacting are the tasks of conceptualizing God's plan as it develops over our confessional heritage, and of portraying imaginatively the reality of the creative, redemptive God in images which give faithful and powerful expression to our faith. The many members preaching, healing, exegeting Scripture, exegeting world, all drawn together into the one body and incarnating the heart and mind of Christ—truly here is an image of the church which remains powerful and promises to guide the church toward a faithful response in action.

Of course, the body of Christ will become incarnate in the life of the church only if the church is true to its Lord, only if the Messiah truly reigns in its midst, only if it yearns to be drawn into the kingdom which is becoming. This brings us back to the need for a dynamic understanding of Scripture, which understanding discerns the creative, redemptive movement originating among our biblical ancestors and flowing through all of reality, which understanding, moreover, hears the Word of God addressing the church today and calling it to enflesh that creative, redemptive movement in the world as the body of Christ.

THE INTERRELATIONSHIP OF THE
TWIN POLARITIES

Before moving to a concrete illustration of the faithful response in action, it will be helpful to add a word of clarification concerning the interrelationship of the form/reform and vision/revision polarities. We can represent that interrelationship as shown in figure 2. The former

FIGURE 2

```
                                                              R
    R                                                         E
    E                                                         V
    F              response                                   I
←-FORM→               in         eschatological         ←-VISION→
    R              action        qualification                I
    M                                                         O
    ↓                                                         N
                                                              ↓
```

polarity aids the church in its search for the faithful response in action
by calling attention to the twin needs of form, order, and security on
the one hand, and those of reform, freedom, and change on the other.
The latter polarity qualifies the former and guards against the tendency
for programs of action to become self-serving, arrogant, and idolatrous,
a temptation perhaps luring many liberal churches in a manner analogous to the temptation of bibliolatry which some conservative groups
face. The vision/revision polarity is thus a reminder of the transcen-
dental reference point to which all earthly institutions and endeavors
must be related and by which they shall all be judged. That reference
point is the eschatological vision of God's kingdom, which while inaugurated by Christ is not yet fulfilled among us. Hence, we must not only
seek to refine earthly forms, but we must strive to clarify our vision of
God's order, which alone can save us from reducing our destiny to
human possibilities and structures.[4] The interrelationship between these
two polarities can help foster a Christian realism about the world. We
work hard at the task of reform, knowing that the God who acts and
the God who becomes incarnate takes the structures of this world seriously. But this work is always conditioned by a dose of pessimism
vis-à-vis the inherent possibilities of worldly structures. We acknowledge
the reality of sin and unveil no programs for human utopias. Perfect-
ibility is not ours. We work at reform, therefore, without illusions of
grandeur. We work simply out of response to divine grace, a grace
which burns the more brilliantly because of the pervasive darkness.

The Lord's Prayer is a perfect example of the tension between the
vision and our call to address pragmatic realities. "Our Father who art
in heaven, hallowed be thy name. Thy kingdom come, thy will be
done . . ." The prayer first focuses on the vision which guides us, which

alone equips us with something to say to the world that goes beyond worldly possibilities. But the supplicant then applies the vision of the kingdom to earthly realities: ". . . on earth as it is in heaven. Give us this day our daily bread, forgive us our trespasses as we forgive those who trespass against us, and lead us not into temptation, but deliver us from evil."

AN ILLUSTRATION OF THE
FAITHFUL RESPONSE IN ACTION

At this point we turn to a specific issue which presses itself upon the church today. By using this issue as an illustration, perhaps we can further clarify the quality of response in action which we feel grows out of a dynamic understanding of Scripture and the church. Intentionally we have chosen one of those complex issues to which the Bible and our confessional heritage as a whole do not offer a simple answer, but in relation to which we nevertheless feel that the church is remiss if it does not respond by viewing all facets of the problem from the perspective of its vision of God's ongoing purposeful activity. For if we in fact believe that all of reality is guided by God according to a righteous plan, that the trajectory of that plan is discernible in our confessional heritage, and that the community of faith lives true to its calling only as it is drawn into that plan, then every pressing social, personal, or global problem must be addressed from within the context of our vision of God's universal purpose. This basis will provide no automatic solutions. In many cases it will add a further dimension of complexity. But we believe that it provides a perspective which is the unique contribution the church has to make to our threatened and fragile modern world.

We shall not, in this illustration, attempt to formulate a solution to the problem. Such a formulation demands far more than the limited knowledge of isolated individuals, for the issues involved are complex. Indeed, responsible action within the church must take the form of an extensive communal effort which elicits the input of a wide range of experts and a broad diversity of opinion.[5] What we seek to do is merely to illustrate how the dynamic understanding of Scripture can contribute to a method of addressing critical problems which is faithful to our confessional heritage and is at the same time in touch with the new realities of a world within which we confess that God is still active in accordance with God's purposes.

Let us then imagine a congregation discussing a working paper from its denominational headquarters on the peaceful use of nuclear energy, especially the generation of electrical power by nuclear reactors. The dynamic view of Scripture we have described and the hermeneutic it implies first of all create a context for the discussion. The context is the community of faith and, more specifically, the church understood as the body of Christ, in which individuals with their various opinions, self-interests, and areas of insight and knowledge are drawn into a purpose that transcends the desires of any individual and derives from a long, collective memory of God's creative, redemptive activity in the world. The ability of the group to rise above the egocentric predicament to address a self-transcending purpose which embraces all of humanity is based on a radical understanding of grace: all that this group is, individually and collectively, is derivative of God's grace. Hence, a sense of gratitude motivates all members to act responsibly and in good faith. For their commitment is single-heartedly to serve God as the body of Christ; and it is the heart and mind of Christ which they as diverse members seek to embody. This unique sense of identity creates a climate of freedom among those reconciled with their God and drawn as brothers and sisters into a common ministry of reconciliation in the world. Individuals do not feel personally threatened as their cherished opinions are challenged by others, for in this setting individual egos are not at stake. Rather, a vision of a kingdom of love, justice, and peace is held up as the self-transcending goal to which all other interests are subservient. In this atmosphere of freedom there is probing, searching, and striving for a faithful response growing out of the best knowledge and wisdom the group is capable of generating.

This open style of dialogue is encouraged by a dynamic understanding of the meaning of Scripture which incorporates the form/reform and the vision/revision polarities. It allows differing perspectives to be understood as expressions of points which are not necessarily exclusive of one another but expressive of different facets of a higher truth than any individual in the group has been able to grasp. In the present discussion dealing with nuclear energy, the form/reform polarity allows the participants to recognize a broad range of needs and considerations arising within a complex society where one decision affects many others. Extreme positions, on either side of the controversy, must relate to questions arising from the need to balance form and reform dimensions. For example, "If all nuclear power plants are banned immediately on account of acknowledged safety hazards, what will be the economic impact on the poor?" Or, "In spite of the economic benefits of nuclear power during a period of energy crisis, what will be the long-range environmental impact?"

The perspective drawn from our scriptural heritage also contributes an important dimension in the form of the visionary/pragmatic or vision/revision polarity. It bases the dialogue of the church on an authority which repudiates co-option by any interest group in the society. For the point of reference is not that of any political party, ideology, business interest, or geographical district but solely a vision of God's intended order of peace wedded with justice for all people in the world. Because this vision itself is not static, however, or tied inalterably to a myth or dogma of the past, but dynamic in its unfolding over the history of God's people, it is a living vision sensitive to the new lessons gained through modern experiment and experience. Thus the vision does not lead to utopianism, for it is constantly translated into pragmatic realities by the living church; nor is it static, for it unfolds according to a notion of God's ongoing purposeful activity.

Within this context of open, searching dialogue grounded on grace and conditioned by the twin polarities, responsible policy on nuclear energy will be sought by the congregation. Involved in its hermeneutic of engagement will be a two-pronged exegesis, exegesis of the confessional heritage and exegesis of the world. The former contributes a deep diachronic dimension by drawing upon the expertise of biblical exegetes, historians of the church, theologians, and ethicists in the effort to relate the central trajectory of the faith to this issue. The latter enlarges the synchronic dimension by enlisting scientists, environmentalists, economists, and any others able to shed light on the problem. Obviously, the magnitude of the issue goes beyond what a single congregation can control, and hence the important role of task forces of the church at large. But the importance of the struggle of the individual congregation and its potential contribution to responsible policy making is never to be minimized.

The possibility of a community transcending its selfish concerns on the basis of its groundedness in grace is enhanced by the eschatological qualification contributed by the vision/revision polarity. No vision of the church is final. God's purpose is the only ultimate reference point. But that will be seen clearly only at the end of history. In the meantime, the vision will be in constant need of revision. This eschatological qualification will help to restrain the drive within leaders to establish their solution as final. Time and again history has witnessed the dogmatic religious posture yield a dogmatic political position. But no community's vision is final. This does not undercut the authoritativeness of the church's vision. It merely places the ultimate source of authority beyond the control of any human individual or group. The result is an openness conducive to receptivity to divine guidance, human reconciliation, and progress toward a peaceful, just world community.

The eschatological perspective afforded by the vision/revision polarity also contributes a prophetic standard. No human standard will serve as substitute for the church's vision of God's intended order of peace and righteousness. Against this standard the church evaluates all policy, and from it the church derives courage to describe the alternatives facing society. In the present energy crisis it resists the temptation to curry the favor of influential politicians or wealthy members of the business community at the expense of honesty. It derives from its millenniums-long heritage of distrust of partial solutions, like minor economic tinkering or a blind trust in the ability of technology to solve all social problems. As agent of a higher standard, it will not be reduced to the role of adding ecclesiastical support to economic or technological answers, but will keep all facets of a problem in mind even as it exposes more serious dimensions of the current social malady, like self-indulgence, greed, and wanton disregard for the welfare of others. The radical perspective of the church is too frequently muted by unholy alliances with powerful leaders of society, the business community, government, and the like, born of the desire to be an acknowledged and esteemed part of the social system. Through such alliances the prophetic task of the church is easily lost. The church becomes just one more institution dedicated to form and resisting the reforming efforts of its prophets. The result is the abdication of its responsibility as steward of a unique vision.

While there is perhaps utility in an illustration such as we have given, ultimately the search for the faithful response in action goes on within the actual community of faith as it relates its vision to the issues and crises of the world like nuclear energy, world hunger, Arab-Israeli relations, boat people, or the imprisonment of political dissidents. Thus our example has been carried as far as we can take it—to the point not of even suggesting a solution but only of illustrating the manner in which an incarnational model of community and a dynamic understanding of

Scripture create a distinct style of addressing a problem. While not suggesting that the church is thereby enabled to answer all questions, and even labeling such an arrogant attitude as an ungodly triumphalism, we nevertheless may question whether our nation by now might not have evolved a much more effective and just energy policy or, for that matter, policy on Indochina or the Middle East, if the church had courageously kept alive in our society a clear image of God's people as a servant people rather than as world masters. How differently the message of the church would sound in Washington, Jerusalem, Tehran, and Pretoria if leaders and laity alike incarnated a living dedication to a vision of God's kingdom of peace wedded with righteousness. Gone would be equivocation born of earlier complicity with unrighteousness. Gone would be duplicity born of a greater concern for our personal standard of living than for the rights of the starving to our surplus. In a world calling for more hard, well-reasoned choices than ever before, the church must embody the heart and mind of Christ. For then it can bring those possessing expert knowledge of Bible and theology together with those possessing expert knowledge of world, and it can center both on a unifying vision of God's purpose. But to do so mandates radical change in the church's priorities and its sense of dedication and mission.

THE FAITHFUL RESPONSE IN ACTION AND INDIVIDUAL RESPONSIBILITY

Throughout our discussion, emphasis has been placed on the church as community. In this chapter, therefore, the faithful response in action has been viewed largely as a corporate response, as the church incarnates its vision of God's kingdom in its role as servant and body of Christ. But we must keep in mind that the body of Christ consists of individual members, each of whom carries before God the responsibility to respond faithfully in his or her own life. Luther spoke of the Christian being a "little Christ" to the neighbor. The incarnational model must be that which structures the personal lives of individual Christians if the corporate church is to be true to its mission as body of Christ in the world.

The church today badly needs leaders who possess a clear and compelling vision of God's unfolding plan of a kingdom wedding universal peace and justice in order that all members of the community of faith may be mindful of their individual responsibility to embody the vision.

On Good Friday 1980, twelve years and a day after one of the most outstanding of our modern church leaders was gunned down on a motel balcony in Memphis, Ralph Abernathy remembered the prophet Martin Luther King, Jr., together with his vision and its Source: "They may have been successful in killing the dreamer but not the dream." How does the dream survive so powerfully in spite of its many detractors and enemies? By "the power of God's divine purpose and plan," Dr. Abernathy explained, as he compared his friend and fellow minister to "another dreamer whose name was Jesus."[6]

Lest the focus on world problems and complex issues perplex individual believers into a moral paralysis which would negate the possibility of a faithful response, it is well to remember that we equip ourselves for addressing large problems by practicing the translation of the central dynamic of Scripture in our everyday personal lives. Each Christian, therefore, is to have the heart and the mind of Christ, for only then can the church, whose many members constitute the body of Christ, incarnate Christ's mission of reconciliation. Therefore, we must honestly face the ways in which our lives contradict the vision of God's kingdom, we who live as kings and rulers on the earth, this fragile home which is incapable of supporting more than a fraction of the human family on the level to which we have grown accustomed. To insist that we be entitled to go on living at such a level contradicts a theme which has developed at the heart of our confessional heritage, namely, that God shows no favorites in the administration of justice and shalom.

We return, therefore, for a moment to our illustration, and imagine those involved in the congregational discussion on energy taking their insights home with the intention of relating them to their personal response in faith. Their reflecting could be guided by what Sister Marie Augusta Neal has called a "theology of relinquishment," which she commends to the nonpoor as a way of thought corresponding to a "theology of liberation" among the poor.[7] In the law of the jubilee and in Deut. 24:10, "what is made clear is that no right of ownership supersedes human need." Therefore, "relinquishing one's claim to what others need is clearly a Gospel mandate."[8] "Sin, accordingly, must be associated with retaining goods that the poor need for survival."[9]

We need to learn the simpler, carefree life of the kingdom, described so well in the Sermon on the Mount (Matt. 6:19–34).[10] And our vision needs to be revised through interaction with those whom our overindulgence and accumulation have compelled to live in want, including minorities within our own society, members of the developing nations, and the poor throughout the world. For example, we need to learn that form, order, and security are not established by amassing a disproportionate share of the earth's resources, and that a concern for the reform of economic inequities is actually a far more dependable servant of stability. Many accordingly are beginning to envision as a part of the faithful response a simpler, more austere life style. In a world of dwindling energy sources, they are learning that walking is to be preferred over driving, that simple times at home are more enjoyable and conducive to deepening friendship than constant activity, that the warmth of a wood stove in an otherwise chilly home can draw the family closer together. As enrichment of the spiritual life through the study of the Word, meditation, and prayer leads to a quieter, more centered life, such believers are experiencing a wonderful transformation: their needs are reduced, they withdraw from the endless futility of laying up "treasures on earth," and they discover more time and means to share in a world of deepening need.

As Sister Marie Augusta emphasizes, our response to the poor must never be narrowed to the realm of personalistic piety, for the problems involved are so vast as to require joint effort. But the personal life is the training ground for members of the church who then corporately address the crises of this world. Thus the vision of God's kingdom of universal justice and peace calls *every* Christian to conform to the new life inaugurated by Christ. And that life is a life of sharing. It prompts Christians to seek ways, individually and as a church, in the personal life and in public planning, to translate the vision in ever broader circles toward the coming of the kingdom in its fullness (Isa. 65:17–25). Their words and their actions thereby express the yearning of their hearts for the day when all God's family will be united under one Lord; when hunger and want will be unknown; when caring, justice, and love will be freely given and freely received by all. To declare such a kingdom an impossible utopia is to repudiate the faithful response in action. But for the individual Christian and the church to commit life and resources to that vision is to participate in God's reign and to announce the inclusion of all God's family in the plan which had been unfolding from the beginning of time.

CHAPTER 7

The Bible

A Call to a Living

and Responsive Faith

Those who are drawn into the purposes of the living God are compelled by no authority other than the self-giving love of God. Among God's gifts they cherish the Bible as the unique collection of narratives and confessions which traces the creative and redemptive movement of God through the ages. And through the Bible they are addressed by the living God, whose nature and will is revealed to them intimately in the paradigmatic events, especially the event of Christ. But they avoid every attempt to imprison the God of mystery within dogmatic systems or within the cult of bibliolatry. God remains sovereign, and the Christian's allegiance is to God alone.

Not all will find convincing what we have called a dynamic view of Scripture. We have observed how this view understands the Bible as testimony to the living Word of God, which Word addresses each generation anew in its concrete setting and calls for the faithful response of incarnating the vision of God's unfolding kingdom within the realities of the modern world. Many continue to look to religion for definitive answers to the questions raised by world events and individual experiences and want to be given a Bible which commends specific solutions rather than a vision of God's kingdom and a life dedicated to incarnating that vision amid reflection and struggle. The notion of a living Word which draws the church into an ongoing creative and redemptive process and which places each generation of the faithful within polarities that necessitate struggle and searching will threaten brittle conceptions of faith. But this is totally understandable, for what human whose goals do not transcend self seeks more tension in an already troubled world? The natural person, acting on purely human, pragmatic principles, will look to religion as a means of avoiding, not enhancing, tension and struggle. "Do not think that I have come to bring peace on earth; I have not come to bring peace, but a sword" (Matt. 10:34). This is an incomprehensible word to all but those who share the vision of the new being, the vision which informs the faithful that the one "who loses . . . life for my sake will find it" (Matt. 10:39b).

Those, however, who have seen the vision of God's kingdom, which is becoming, experience a call to a living and responsive faith which regards struggle and tension as a natural part of taking the cross and following the Lord. For they are guided by a transcendent vision and are dedicated to translating that vision into the realities of a suffering and sinful world. They are guided by a living Word which addresses them as a body of Christ and calls them to incarnate God's purposes in everyday life. Within a relationship that is living and growing they accept the interaction of vision with world—or what we have called the dialectic of faith—as an essential aspect of a partnership which is vital and genuine. Within the dialectic of faith, moreover, polarities like that of form/reform and vision/translation foster an openness to God's initiative and a commitment to faithful response in every particular situation. This response calls for no simple repetition of scripts from the past. For the new covenant into which the church has been drawn is a covenant not externally imposed on passive recipients but one received as a gift from the living God, understood on the basis of the confessional heritage, and experienced anew within the everyday affairs of life.

As students of Scripture who both accept the legitimacy of critical biblical scholarship and find such scholarship supportive of the church's mission, we have a message which we should like to see debated openly among Christians holding various points of view. When absorbed in the self-transcending purpose of God and thus delivered from the hubris which has plagued the field, theological study of the Bible which makes full use of all available tools can foster a dynamic understanding of the Bible as God's living Word, a Word which addresses the church and draws it into the creative, redemptive drama which is vividly charted within the pages of the Bible. Within this understanding, thoughtful minds are not forced to conform to archaic formulations, but as minds embodying the mind of Christ they are invited to incarnate God's plan as it now moves forth in the world. Within this understanding, full hearts moved by compassion in the sight of a suffering, starving world are not obliged to restrict love's response to ancient prescriptions and ordinances but are urged to embody the heart of Christ in the new response which dares to go beyond the old, even as God continues to inaugurate the new. Here courage is necessary, for love's mandate is not as "safe" as the dictates chiseled in stone. Minds and hearts prompted by a love so lavish as the divine love manifested in Christ will not falter, however, but will search for the faithful response out of gratitude and commitment. And they will be led by a trustworthy guide, a three-thousand-year history, and the vivid paradigms of faith! Within this living relationship with God, to stand up for the poor against powerful oppressors, to strive for equal distribution of the earth's resources, to foster honesty and love in all relationships are not just stipulations. They are aspects of the church's and the individual's growth into the body of Christ and into the new creation. And as manifestations of the embodiment of the heart and mind of Christ, they have profound ontological significance: they are signs of the growth of creation toward the wholeness which God intends for all!

APPENDIX

The Important Contributions
of Current
Liberation Movements

In the chapters of this book, it has been presupposed that the new insights into God's purpose to which we try to remain open come primarily among those presently struggling in God's name against oppression. Most of us are unable to compose the new exodus narrative or paint the new image of the God of the oppressed. But the polarities of faith described in this book, it is hoped, will help to keep all of us open to the new narratives and images as they arise among the suffering servants of God.

Aware of the partiality of my own vision in relation to women's concerns, I append here a previously published essay on one problem facing women as they seek to relate to their scriptural heritage, the problem of sexist language.[1] I wish I could go further in a dialogue with feminist concerns, and expand this dialogue to include concerns of Blacks, Hispanics, and Central and South American liberationists. In the hope that such an occasion may arise, I shall try in the meantime to remain open to the visions of others arising from their struggles on battlefields where faith can discern the activity of the gracious God of all people.

MASCULINE METAPHORS FOR GOD
AND SEX DISCRIMINATION
IN THE OLD TESTAMENT

Two Views of Scriptural Authority

Before we enter the topic of biblical metaphor, we should clarify our view of scriptural authority. There are two vastly differing views current among Christians. One regards the Bible as a collection of timeless truths and immutable laws dictated by God and recorded by humans.

136

Christian behavior is determined by application of these truths and laws to the contemporary life of the believer and the Christian community. For example, if Scripture admonishes women to remain silent and cover their heads in worship, the requirement is binding upon women in the contemporary church. The system has the advantage of being straightforward and direct, though the appearance of being free from dangers of rationalization is tarnished by the fact that while such laws as the above are legalistically upheld, countless ceremonial laws claiming equal Mosaic or apostolic authority are ignored. Furthermore, the forced interpretations devised to cover matters not treated in Scripture, for example, birth control and abortion, are unsatisfying. More troublesome, however, is the suspicion that a cutting edge in Scripture is dulled when regulations permitting slavery and laws discriminating between the relative rights of individuals on the basis of gender are ascribed the same degree of authority as divine acts directed at freeing slaves and demolishing power structures used to oppress nonadvantaged segments of society.

We are led to a second view, therefore, which regards the Bible as an historical record of a group of people which draws attention by means of confessional formulations to a liberating dynamic within the historical process, a dynamic variously called Yahweh, Elohim, or Adonai. The various parts of that scriptural record must be interpreted in relation to that liberating dynamic.

Central Issues Growing from the
Relation of Biblical Metaphors
to Gender Discrimination

THE DOMINANCE OF THE MALE METAPHOR

The dominance of the male metaphor in designations of the Deity is no mere historical accident of indifference in the discussion of sex discrimination in biblical religion. It is the product, not of a society which could freely choose the gender of its primary metaphors, but of a society driven to choose male metaphors by virtue of patriarchal structures predicated upon sexual inequality. Moreover, these male metaphors have been taken up—in what must seem to women to be a conspiracy spanning three millenniums—by contemporary males in another systematic discrimination against women deeply rooted in societal structures. This discrimination reverberates through family role differentiation, professional promotion systems, political and social structures, and ecclesiastical orders. We conclude, therefore, that the gender of the biblical metaphor is not a matter of indifference to those women who find it difficult or impossible to relate positively to male metaphors for the Deity which are used by their male contemporaries (let's face it, and use the term *male superiors*!) to further oppress them in the name of the same male deity used by men in biblical times to safeguard their patriarchal privileges.

THE BIBLICAL GOD AS ENEMY OF OPPRESSIVE POWER STRUCTURES AND AS A CHAMPION OF THE OPPRESSED

While the question of gender and biblical metaphor is important, it cannot be the sole focus of a discussion attempting to treat the relation of biblical metaphor to sex discrimination. This we shall illustrate by a contrast.

Example A. The Canaanite religious system which preceded Yahwism in Palestine was replete with goddesses alongside the patriarchal gods. Rooted in concerns with fertility, this system accorded a position of great importance, for example, to Anath, sister of Baal. She needed to take second position to no male warrior in her day of battle:

> Now Anath doth battle in the plain,
>   Fighting between the two towns;
> Smiting the Westland's peoples,
>   Smashing the folk of the Sunrise.
> Under her, heads like sheaves;
>   Over her, hands like locusts,
>   Like a grass-hopper-mass heroes' hands.
> She binds the heads to her back,
>   Fastens the hands in her girdle.
> She plunges knee-deep in knight's blood,
>   Hip-deep in the gore of heroes.
>   (Ancient Near Eastern Texts, p. 136)

We have, moreover, evidence of the goddess Astarte's popularity among the folk in hundreds of plaques found throughout Palestine in the Early Bronze Age. But the dominant presence of the female metaphor alone does not bespeak the liberated position of women in that society. This is seen in the fact that both male and female deities of the Canaanite pantheon lived on a level far below that of the humans of that society, judging from a comparison between the myths and the laws. More importantly, however, is the function of the myths in general in the Canaanite cult. They functioned to legitimize the existing power structures presided over by the king, power structures within which the subordinate positions of women and slaves were tied to the eternal realities revealed by the myth. That is to say, the myths were a deification of those power structures. The de facto debased position of the woman in such societies is illustrated in a description by Herodotus of the mother goddess cult in Babylon (Aphrodite is the equivalent of Anath in Canaan):

> The foulest Babylonian custom is that which compels every woman of the land once in her life to sit in the temple of Aphrodite and have intercourse with some stranger. Many women who are rich and proud and disdain to consort with the rest, drive to the temple in covered carriages drawn by teams and there stand with a great retinue of attendants. But most sit down in the sacred plot of Aphrodite, with crowns of cord on their heads; there is a great multitude of women coming and going; passages marked by line run every way through the crowd, by which stranger men pass and make their choice. When a woman has once taken her place there she goes not away to her home before some stranger has cast money into her lap and had intercourse with her outside the temple; but while he casts the money, he must say, "I demand thee in the name of Mylitta" (that is the Assyrian name of Aphrodite). It matters not what be the sum of the money; the woman will never refuse, for that were a sin, the money by this act made sacred. So she follows the first man who casts it and rejects none. After their intercourse she has made herself holy in the goddess's sight and goes away to her home; and thereafter there is no bribe however great that will get her. So then the women that are fair and tall are soon free to depart, but the uncomely have long to wait because they cannot fulfil the law; for some of them remain for three years, or four. There is a custom like to this in some parts of Cyprus.
>
> (I, 199)

Though the dominant metaphor in this cult is feminine, it is dedicated to a view of woman which reduces her to a sex object (as the fertility plaques with their exaggerated representations of the breasts and genitals illustrate), thereby thrusting life into a debased one-dimensionality. It is important to recognize here that while such cults were dedicated to a goddess, they were still a part of male-dominated social structures. The dominance of a female metaphor is thus no guarantee of sexual equality.

Example B. In Yahwism, a monotheistic tendency coupled with an historicism which deemphasized the fertility myth edged out the female metaphor and led to the domination of male metaphors for the Deity. But at the same time, while seemingly removing women even further from religious and social equality, it broke the control of myth as the legitimizer of the oppressive power structures presided over by the absolute monarch. Introduced thereby was a latent potentiality for liberation from the shackles of oppressive power structures, the full dynamism of which still remains unharnessed. We turn now to develop this point.

The Function of Religion as Guarantor of the Power Structures of the Absolute Monarch Challenged and Broken

Both Palestine and Egypt in the Late Bronze Age (ca. fifteenth to fourteenth centuries) were regulated by royal structures legitimized by a mythopoeic system. Social structures, whether they related to the status of king or free person, slave or woman, were eternally guaranteed by the mythic realities. Outside those social structures were the *'apiru,* disenfranchised individuals who had renounced the king and thereby declared themselves unregulated by the royal myth (*'apiru = habiru =* Hebrew).[2] A group of slaves in Egypt joined the ranks of the *'apiru* when Moses intervened in an act condoned by the social system, the beating of a Hebrew by an Egyptian. Moses' act of killing the Egyptian was tantamount to pronouncing: "I declare myself unbound by the social system and its legitimizing myth. Hereafter, I am an *'apiru*." This defiant act was followed by the corporate act of defiance on the part of the Hebrew slaves under Moses' leadership. Their rebellion and escape violated the myth of the state. The consequence should have been divine punishment inflicted by the Pharaoh upon the rebels. That the opposite occurred called the legitimacy of the myth into question. From the Hebrews' perspective, divine power had not sided with the absolute monarch so as to preserve his oppressive power structures; it had sided with the slaves in their rebellion against those purported eternal, inviolable structures. The seeds of a new religious myth had been sown. Its protagonists were not priests and kings but slaves, newly emancipated by what they interpreted as an act of God. According to their inchoate myth, God was the champion of the oppressed, and God was active in the events of everyday life to deliver the helpless. The focus of religion was redirected dramatically away from the sacred, timeless space of myth to the profane, ongoing processes of history.

A period ensued in which those 'apiru sought to define the new quality of life they had experienced in their myth; this they attempted in the recitation of historical events in which they detected the liberating dynamic they called Yahweh, as well as in the formulation of various laws guaranteeing the egalitarian rights of each individual. It is noteworthy that the documents of this early, formative period are filled with songs and deeds of heroic women: "And Miriam sang to them: / 'Sing to the Lord, for he has triumphed gloriously; / the horse and his rider he has thrown into the sea'" (Exod. 15:21). (Only later did editors replace Miriam with Moses in Exod. 15:1.)

> The peasantry ceased in Israel, they ceased
>   until you arose, Deborah,
>   arose as a mother in Israel.
>   (Judg. 5:7)

> Most blessed of women be Jael,
>   the wife of Heber the Kenite,
>   of tent-dwelling women most blessed.
> He asked water, and she gave him milk,
>   she brought him curds in a lordly bowl.
> She put her hand to the tent peg
>   and her right hand to the workmen's mallet;
> she struck Sisera a blow,
>   she crushed his head,
>   she shattered and pierced his temple.
> He sank, he fell,
>   he lay still at her feet;
> at her feet he sank, he fell;
>   where he sank, there he fell dead.
>   (Judg. 5:24–27)

The social implications of this new slave myth of the God who destroys the myths and social structures of the powerful and who, in the events of history, frees and blesses the oppressed, are drawn in a song of another woman, Hannah:

> Hannah also prayed and said,
> "My heart exults in the Lord;
>   my strength is exalted in the Lord.
> My mouth derides my enemies,
>   because I rejoice in thy salvation.

"There is none holy like the Lord,
  there is none besides thee;
  there is no rock like our God.
Talk no more so very proudly,
  let not arrogance come from your mouth;
for the Lord is a God of knowledge,
  and by him actions are weighed.
The bows of the mighty are broken,
  but the feeble gird on strength.
Those who were full have hired themselves out for bread,
  but those who were hungry have ceased to hunger.
The barren has borne seven,
  but she who has many children is forlorn.
The Lord kills and brings to life;
  he brings down to Sheol and raises up.
The Lord makes poor and makes rich;
  he brings low, he also exalts.
He raises up the poor from the dust;
  he lifts the needy from the ash heap,
to make them sit with princes
  and inherit a seat of honor.
For the pillars of the earth are the Lord's,
  and on them he has set the world."

                                          (1 Sam. 2:1–8)

The New Liberation Dynamic
Poured into Canaanite
(That Is, Socially Conditioned,
Sexist) Vessels

   The Book of the Covenant (Exod. 20:22—23:19) is the earliest collection of laws in the Bible (ca. eleventh century B.C.). It illustrates both the attempts of former slaves to safeguard their newly won equality and the stubborn resilience of customs and laws from the discarded social system that keep reemerging, thereby threatening the viability of the new equality. Regarding the former quality, consider the following:

   You shall not wrong a stranger or oppress him, for you were strangers in the land of Egypt. You shall not afflict any widow or orphan. If you do afflict them, and they cry out to me, I will surely hear their cry; and my wrath will burn, and I will kill you with the sword, and your wives shall become widows and your children fatherless.
   If you lend money to any of my people with you who is poor, you shall not be to him as a creditor, and you shall not exact interest from him. If ever you take your neighbor's garment in pledge, you shall re-

store it to him before the sun goes down; for that is his only covering, it is his mantle for his body; in what else shall he sleep? And if he cries to me, I will hear, for I am compassionate.

(Exod. 22:21–27)

Here measures are taken to assure that the abuses earlier suffered by the Hebrews in Egypt are not in turn inflicted by the Hebrews upon aliens in their midst: exploitation of strangers is forbidden, "for you were strangers in the land of Egypt." The widows and orphans, representing two other helpless classes in the society, are also protected by law, with the assurance that Yahweh is the Champion of the oppressed: "If you do afflict them, and they cry out to me, I will surely hear their cry; and my wrath will burn, and I will kill you with the sword." Finally, the Israelite is not to assume the role of creditor by exacting interest and withholding a garment taken in pledge, "for this is his only covering, it is his mantle for his body; in what else shall he sleep? And if he cries to me, I will hear, for I am compassionate." We witness here a truly remarkable set of laws, giving flesh and heart to a community impregnated by the liberating dynamic of a God who protects the stranger from exploitation, defends the widow and orphan, and safeguards the rights of the indebted poor.

But how can it be that within the same collection of laws, the emancipation of male slaves is legislated (21:1–6), but "when a man sells his daughter as a slave, she shall not go out as the male slaves do" (21:7)? How can it be that the Defender of the widow and the orphan is credited with laws in which a man can treat a woman as his chattel (21:22–24; 22:16)?

This juxtaposition of liberation dynamic and perpetuation of discriminating laws and customs greatly complicates the interpretation of the Bible in relation to sex discrimination. A clear distinction must be drawn between, on the one hand, the liberation dynamic which former slaves recognized in their experiences and which they attempted to articulate in credo and embody in law, and on the other, discriminating laws and customs drawn from their environment. Our ever-increasing knowledge of the ancient Near Eastern world proves that it was a slaveholding, sex-discriminating society within which Hebrew slaves and women discovered the saving activity of Yahweh on their behalf. But when they came to record and transmit that saving activity, they poured its dynamism into socially conditioned vehicles which themselves were discriminatory: slave laws and sexist customs and metaphors. Thus arose a harsh contradiction between the liberation dynamic and the vehicles of expression to which that dynamic was accommodated.

But are we deluding ourselves with such subtle distinctions? Is not the distinction between liberation dynamic and socially conditioned vehicles of expression double talk—rationalization devised to salvage a contradictory religious system which greater courage and honesty would discard? The fact that some liberationists, including feminists, would reply in the affirmative underscores the seriousness of this question. And to them our reply will perhaps be further subtle rationalizing. For we would suggest that the fact that biblical religion was developed, not in the sacred space of the temple, but in the secular realm of the everyday, categorically required that "Canaanite" vessels be used. Our historical interpretation of biblical religion leads us to maintain that the view that Mosaic law was imposed by divine dictation through a passive scribe holding a chisel and two stones is a later mythologization. Yahweh the Defender of slaves and widows dawned on the 'apiru within historical events of the sort experienced by moderns as well. Therefore, of necessity, that dawning occurred amid customs and mind-sets which were patriarchal in a patriarchal society. It also involved an infusion of a liberation dynamic into laws, customs, idioms, myths, and metaphors which were not only inadequate as vehicles of the new ideal but were often downright contradictory and hostile. And it is therefore not the purity of the formulations of the biblical epics, laws, and customs which motivates us in our search for liberation, but the very contradictions resident therein, for it is in the *contradiction* that we hear the tradition cry out for liberating activity which will continue to attack power structures that oppress and destroy. Within the very customs and laws of our tradition which have molded us these contradictions between liberation and oppression coexist. Is it any wonder we are torn and restless, both as individuals and as a community? And we should beware of the opponents of the contradiction, for they seek to banish the liberation dynamic in order to establish an ordered structure which can restore peace in a torn society, at the expense of further oppression. Let us not fear the pain of dissension so much as the perfect order the eternal myth sponsored. In fact, when the well-ordered society emerges, let us not hesitate to invite back the contradictions which leave room for the God who attacks power structures on behalf of the oppressed and which burst forth with hostile force precisely when priests or kings or dictators or dominant males have seemingly turned God into a reliable legitimizer of their myth of elitism and superiority.

Former Slaves Transform Their New Power into New Structures of Oppression

Power often corrupts. The powerful have great difficulty in seeking first God's kingdom and his righteousness. History has repeated this lesson continually. The compromise imposed upon the newly experienced liberation dynamic by the Canaanite vessels was nothing in comparison to the full-fledged system of elitism, discrimination, and oppression reestablished in Israel by Solomon. Persecuted and hunted prophets and exploited, powerless poor people provided the only ground in Israel where the liberation ideal could be nurtured. Appropriately, it finally found its most effective metaphor in the figure of a leprous prophet:

> Who has believed what we have heard?
>   And to whom has the arm of the Lord been revealed?
> For he grew up before him like a young plant,
>   and like a root out of dry ground;
> he had no form or comeliness that we should look at him,
>   and no beauty that we should desire him.
> He was despised and rejected by men;
>   a man of sorrows, and acquainted with grief;
> and as one from whom men hide their faces
>   he was despised, and we esteemed him not.
>   (Isa. 53:1–3)

In the very weakness of this despised person God was active to save the weak:

> Surely he has borne our griefs
>   and carried our sorrows;
> yet we esteemed him stricken,
>   smitten by God, and afflicted.
> But he was wounded for our transgressions,
>   he was bruised for our iniquities;
> upon him was the chastisement that made us whole,
>   and with his stripes we are healed.
>   (Isa. 53:4–5)

Until this revolutionary metaphor was invented by Second Isaiah, the liberation ideal was transmitted primarily in the metaphor of a fierce, bloody, "holy" warrior, taken from the very mythic system the Hebrews had broken from, and itself representing a bitter contradiction between the new liberation ideal and media of expression. Exceptions to this metaphor are noteworthy but not numerous (for example, Hos. 11:1-9; Ezekiel 23; Zech. 12:10-14). But the metaphor of the servant who becomes an instrument of liberation not through a destructive show of force but through vicarious suffering is a remarkable new chapter indeed in the history of the biblical liberation dynamic. For all along, its most astonishing message was that divine presence is to be discovered among the suffering and the oppressed. How appropriate now that precisely in a suffering servant God's saving activity is discerned.

The next radical step was taken when God him/herself was identified with the suffering servant. In Jesus, God was seen as not only acting *through* a suffering prophet but as *entering* into the suffering of the oppressed. Oppressive power structures are not here destroyed by a powerful divine explosion, but by a miracle of resurrection occurring through full identification with the powerless and oppressed.

Biblical Metaphor in Relation to Oppressive Power Structures Today

Once again the liberation dynamic, present in the liberated 'apiru community, in the persecuted prophets, in Jesus, in oppressed and hunted opponents of the exploitation of the powerful crying in the wilderness of subsequent centuries, is neatly "contained" within dogmatic systems presided over by religionists who are lackeys of the powerful. No wonder many women waking up to their oppression resent a religion presided over by men using the masculine metaphors of the tradition to abort the liberation dynamic impregnating those metaphors. No wonder they detect that such deception is no different from the slaveholder's use of the Book of the Covenant to transform Yahweh, the Deliverer of slaves, into Jehovah, the upholder of slave laws. To some such women, it is inevitable that the masculine metaphors are a tremendous obstacle to worship and appreciation of biblical tradition. The first level of the problem must be dealt with, and there are ways. Not only can biblical translations reflect a new sensitivity, but we should possess enough imagination in our contemporary application of biblical metaphors to draw upon the fullness of human experience in giving expression to the ineffable God, rather than restricting our usage to the experience of the one-half of society which also happens to be guilty of the most ungodly acts of oppression and exploitation.

In addition to the question of the gender of the metaphor is the rediscovery of a liberation dynamic within the sexist, discriminatory language which is able to break through the dogmatic crust provided by the priests and kings dedicated to elimination of the contradiction. Here is a task in which biblical scholarship must strain to be true to the prophetic tradition, that of reexamining the contradiction, desacralizing the "vessels" in order that the uncontainable God may be free to attack the very power structures which for so long have been able to silence this Creator and Liberator. The metaphors in themselves are not sacred. They are often derived from the very structures they are commissioned to destroy. We must not so focus upon the vessels that we fail to recognize in our tradition and in our contemporary life the Liberator who spoke through Second Isaiah:

> Remember not the former things,
>   nor consider the things of old.
> Behold, I am doing a new thing;
>   now it springs forth, do you not perceive it?
>   (Isa. 43:18–19)

What a surprise our biblical tradition holds for contemporary oppressors: the very metaphors they find so useful in exploiting the weak contain the revolutionary dynamic to destroy their oppressive power base.

Here my exploratory suggestions must end, for the history of our biblical tradition teaches us another lesson: it is not the establishment representative of an exploitative society who finally exposes the revolutionary liberating dynamic inherent within a religious tradition, or who discovers fresh metaphors capable of infusing individuals with vitality to become actors in the drama of new creation; that exposure and discovery comes rather from the groups discriminated against and exploited by the establishment; it comes from the very passion of their liberation struggles. As a white male in a sexist society, therefore, I must repentantly accept my place among those who need more to be taught than to teach, whose hopes for rediscovering their own true humanity are tied to their recapturing a vision of God's liberating activity through the eyes of those who have experienced the presence of the ineffable One who "raises up the poor from the dust," and "lifts the needy from the ash heap."

Notes

PREFACE

1. The element of playfulness in biblical study has been described exquisitely by Father Raymond Brown in a discussion treating accommodation: "Finally, even pure accommodation is not without value. Even though it is not a scriptural sense, it may be a pleasant and useful means of spiritual progress. After all, in the Scriptures we are in our Father's house where the children are permitted to play." Raymond E. Brown, *The Sensus Plenior* (Baltimore: St. Mary's University, 1955), p. 28.

CHAPTER 1. THE BIBLE: THE LANGUAGE OF A LIVING RELATIONSHIP

1. Though the concept of polarity sometimes bears negative connotations, it is the most useful term I know to describe the interrelatedness of important qualities like form and reform, or vision and revision, in the Bible. Connoted is a positive kind of tension which is conducive to a dynamic posture in which the faithful are open to divine direction. Our recognition of polarities in the Bible also accords well with our confession that in Scripture we relate to a God of holy mystery who is beyond our comprehension, yet who has chosen to be revealed to us in the events of history and in the stuff of human experience. Polarities allow us to describe the dynamism and richness of divine revelation without the danger of reducing diverse manifestation to a pale, systematic consistency. Important work has been done on the concept of polarity by Hans (Jean) Gebser, *Ursprung und Gegenwart*, 2 vols. (Stuttgart: Deutsche Verlags-Anstalt, 1949–53). Other terms have been applied to the study of diverse streams in the Bible. Walter Brueggemann, for example, has applied the trajectory concept to distinct traditions which can be traced through the religion of Israel ("Trajectories in Old Testament Literature and the Sociology of Ancient Israel," *Journal of Biblical Literature* 98 [1979]: 161–85). In this book, we shall use the term "trajectory" to designate the development of a dynamic concept of divine activity spanning the entire history of our confessional heritage.

148

2. An emphatic statement of this position is developed in Harold Lindsell, *The Battle for the Bible* (Grand Rapids, Mich.: Zondervan Publishing House, 1976).

3. The traditional position is described vividly by Hans Frei in *The Eclipse of Biblical Narrative* (New Haven: Yale University Press, 1974), pp. 1–3.

4. Friedrich Schleiermacher, *Hermeneutics: The Handwritten Manuscripts,* American Academy of Religion, Texts and Translations 1, ed. H. Kimmerle, trans. J. Duke and J. Forstman (Missoula, Mont.: Scholars Press, 1977), p. 111.

5. Martin Heidegger, *An Introduction to Metaphysics,* trans. R. Manheim (New Haven: Yale University Press, 1959), p. 13.

6. This concern has deep roots in the thought of Schleiermacher and Dilthey. A fine study on the subject is Richard E. Palmer's *Hermeneutics: Interpretation Theory in Schleiermacher, Dilthey, Heidegger, and Gadamer* (Evanston, Ill.: Northwestern University Press, 1969).

7. Hans-Georg Gadamer, *Truth and Method* (New York: Seabury Press, 1975).

8. One can scarcely be too careful in trying to preserve the many facets included in a biblical understanding of events as acts of God. In *Dynamic Transcendence: The Correlation of Confessional Heritage and Contemporary Experience in a Biblical Model of Divine Activity* (Philadelphia: Fortress Press, 1978) I tried to show how a revelatory event includes four elements, each essential if the richness of our biblical heritage is to be preserved: (1) confessional heritage, (2) objective happenings, (3) the living faith of the community in its worship and service of God, and (4) the new confessional response. Apparently I did not emphasize the third element sufficiently, for one reviewer (Christopher B. Kaiser, *Reformed Review* [1979]: 43–4) writes: "The basic dialectic of 'new event' and 'confessional heritage' is then developed into a schematic view of salvation history (diagrams are provided) that is well worth studying; it is the best treatment of the subject since Oscar Cullmann's *Salvation in History* (Harper and Row, 1967). From what I have already relayed, however, one can see the basic problem with Hanson's approach: it is really an immanentist view of history that could be used by a humanist or a Marxist, as well as by a Christian or a Jew, provided the occasional references to 'God' were omitted."

In order to clarify that I am not proposing an immanentist view of history, I shall quote from p. 52 of *Dynamic Transcendence:* "In addition, to avoid a rationalizing reductionism which would describe as incidental human hypothesis the emergence of confession out of the confluence of confessional heritage and new event, it is essential to recognize as part of the divine act the reality of the living faith of the community as a revelatory matrix animated by communion with the divine *Mysterium.*"

Further to this point is footnote 7 to chapter 5 of the same book (p. 100–101): "This dynamic view of divine activity should not be confused with pantheistic views which identify God with historical process. Stated positively, our view describes God as the Purposer to whom alone can be attributed the meaningful pattern unifying all reality in its diverse facets, whether historical, cosmic, or communal. Whenever we speak, therefore, of the structural pattern underlying a web of objective circumstances and happenings, or of the dynamic and creative force of the confessional heritage, or of the response of the community of faith, we are describing activity directed by a God active in but not limited by historical phenomena." Elsewhere in that book, I point out that while the living experience of God's presence is the most difficult to describe in a model of biblical events as acts of God, this existential moment is essential and central to any understanding of biblical revelation.

CHAPTER 2. KINGS AND PROPHETS IN TENSION, AND THE DEVELOPMENT OF THE FORM/REFORM POLARITY

1. Harold Lindsell, *The Battle for the Bible* (Grand Rapids, Mich: Zondervan Publishing House, 1976).

2. Certain of the themes developed in the remainder of this chapter were treated in the author's "Prophets and Kings," *Humanitas* 15 (1979): 287–303.

3. The interaction between a cosmic vector and a teleological vector in the Bible has been treated in the author's *Dynamic Transcendence: The Correlation of Confessional Heritage and Contemporary Experience in a Biblical Model of Divine Activity* (Philadelphia: Fortress Press, 1978).

4. All biblical translations are according to the Revised Standard Version, with the exception of passages from Isaiah 56–66 and Zechariah 9–14, which are from the author's *The Dawn of Apocalyptic*, rev. ed. (Philadelphia: Fortress Press, 1979).

5. For further study of the Book of the Covenant as an important early documentation of the emergent world view of Yahivism, see the author's "The Theological Significance of Contradiction Within the Book of the Covenant," in *Canon and Authority: Essays in Old Testament Religion and Theology*, eds. George W. Coats and Burke O. Long (Philadelphia: Fortress Press, 1977), pp. 110–31. Of great importance for the study of the entire period of the League is Norman Gottwald's book *The Tribes of Yahweh: A Sociology of the Religion of Liberated Israel 1250–1050 B.C.E.* (Maryknoll, N.Y.: Orbis Books, 1979).

6. Phenomena bearing certain resemblances to biblical prophecy are attested in ancient Near Eastern literature, but the differences outweigh the similarities. Most notable is the activity of the *āpilu,* the *assinu,* and the *muhhû* of the Mari documents of the eighteenth century B.C. The relation between the ecstatic outbreak of the servant of Wen-Amon in an Egyptian tale of the eleventh century B.C. and biblical prophecy is even more remote. On these and other parallels, see H. B. Huffmon, "Prophecy in the Ancient Near East," *The Interpreter's Dictionary of the Bible,* Suppl. Vol. (Nashville: Abingdon Press, 1976), pp. 697–700.

7. A vivid description of the struggle between kings and prophets is found in Walter Brueggemann's book *The Prophetic Imagination* (Philadelphia: Fortress Press, 1978).

CHAPTER 3. APOCALYPTIC SEERS AND PRIESTS IN CONFLICT, AND THE DEVELOPMENT OF THE VISIONARY/PRAGMATIC POLARITY

1. Amos Wilder, "Interlude," in *Battle-Retrospect and Other Poems,* The Yale Series of Younger Poets (New Haven: Yale University Press, 1923), p. 31. Used by permission.

2. Alexander Pope, *Essay on Man,* lines 267–76, 285–94.

3. Dietrich Bonhoeffer, *Prayers from Prison: Prayers and Poems* (Philadelphia: Fortress Press, 1978), pp. 17–18.

4. Cited by Eberhard Bethge, *Dietrich Bonhoeffer* (New York: Harper & Row, Publishers, 1970), p. 489.

5. A detailed examination of the Zadokite response can be found in the author's *The Dawn of Apocalyptic,* rev. ed. (Philadelphia: Fortress Press, 1979), pp. 209–79.

6. See chapter 2, note 4, above.

7. Ibid.

8. A more complete account of the visionary response is given in the author's *The Dawn of Apocalyptic,* pp. 32–208 and 280–413.

CHAPTER 4. THE TWIN POLARITIES AS A *PRAEPARATIO* FOR THE MESSIANIC INTERPRETATION OF JESUS' MISSION

1. See the author's *Dynamic Transcendence: The Correlation of Confessional Heritage and Contemporary Experience in a Biblical Model of Divine Activity* (Philadelphia: Fortress Press, 1978).

2. James W. Ward has described the contrast between the royal psalms and the oracles of Isaiah 9 and 11 thus: "In the royal cultus the ethical responsibility of the king was subordinated to his divine right. However, this order of emphasis was reversed in the messianic oracles of Isaiah" (*Amos and Isaiah: Prophets of the Word of God* [Nashville: Abingdon Press, 1969], p. 266).

3. The openness of early Christianity to God's new activity is studied from the perspective offered by the social sciences in John G. Gager's *Kingdom and Community: The Social World of Early Christianity* (Englewood Cliffs, N.J.: Prentice-Hall, 1975). Applying categories like K. Burridge's "new-religions-in-the-making" and P. Berger's "world-construction," Gager draws attention to the conditions creating a millenarian openness to the future. Such study is helpful in clarifying the concrete context within which biblical faith developed, though—as Gager and others utilizing such methods would maintain—results are tentative and never exhaustive. Moreover, they must never obscure the important ties which early Christianity maintained with its Jewish heritage.

4. We use this phrase, derived from Job 40:6 and popularized in Langdon

Gilkey's book by this title, to refer to the theological attempt to understand and conceptualize ultimate reality, that is, God.

5. The theological motif of the *deus absconditus* has recently been given the emphasis it deserves within biblical theology by Samuel Terrien in *The Elusive Presence: Toward a New Biblical Theology* (New York: Harper & Row, Publishers, 1978), for example, pp. 250–52 and 321–26.

CHAPTER 5. THE FAITHFUL RESPONSE (1):
THE INTERPRETATION AND TRANSFORMATION OF
BIBLICAL SYMBOLS

1. We borrow here the title of Peter Berger's thought-provoking book *A Rumor of Angels: Modern Society and the Rediscovery of the Supernatural* (Garden City, N.Y.: Doubleday & Co., 1970). Berger draws from his study this important conclusion: "A rediscovery of the supernatural will be, above all, a regaining of openness in our perception of reality" (p. 95).

2. W. H. Auden, "September 1, 1939," in *Another Time: Poems* (New York: Random House, 1940), pp. 98–101.

3. Douglas J. Hall, *Lighten our Darkness: Toward an Indigenous Theology of the Cross* (Philadelphia: Westminster Press, 1976).

4. The classic critique of the life of Jesus research is still Albert Schweitzer's *The Quest of the Historical Jesus,* trans. W. Montgomery (London: Adam & Charles Black, 1910; New York: Macmillan Co., 1968).

5. We shall describe Sister Marie August Neal's notion of "a theology of relinquishment" in chapter 6.

6. Brita Stendahl, *Sabbatical Reflections: The Ten Commandments in a New Day* (Philadelphia: Fortress Press, 1980), p. 24.

7. "Report of the Task Force on Issues of Biblical Translation" (9 May 1980); and National Council of Churches, Office of News and Information: "National Council of Churches to Consider Inclusive-Language Lectionary," 65 DEM (12 June 1980).

CHAPTER 6. THE FAITHFUL RESPONSE (2):
ACTION WHICH INCARNATES THE LIVING WORD

1. Three guidelines can be identified which describe some of the essential qualities of the communal life lived in harmony with a vision of the unfolding of divine purpose: (1) To live as an historical extension of the biblical community of faith implies a life of givenness to divine purpose. (2) To be guided by the dynamic conveyed by the confessional heritage requires of a community of faith a relationship of critical engagement with that heritage. (3) Fidelity to a biblically based ontology of events draws the responsive community of faith into a life of deep engagement with the issues and events of the contemporary world interpreted as a part of God's ongoing activity. These guidelines, which are elaborated on pp. 77–90 of the author's *Dynamic Transcendence: The Correlation of Confessional Heritage and Contemporary Experience in a Biblical Model of Divine Activity* (Philadelphia: Fortress Press, 1978) certainly are not a complete guide to a biblical hermeneutic,

but they do indicate some of the dynamism which will characterize a community of faith which derives its identity from an understanding of the Bible as "living Word."

2. To use a formulation of Paul Lehmann, *Ethics in a Christian Context* (London: SCM Press, 1963; New York: Harper & Row, Publishers, paper, 1976), p. 85.

3. The diversity of the New Testament is as rich as that of the Old, though exploration of that diversity can be conducted more adequately by New Testament scholars. See, for example, James M. Robinson and Helmut Koester, *Trajectories Through Early Christianity* (Philadelphia: Fortress Press, 1971). Besides the image of the body of Christ, the New Testament offers many others, including "people of God," "house of God," and "temple of God."

4. Peter Berger, from the perspective of sociology, addresses this same point: "The principal moral benefit of religion is that it permits a confrontation with the age in which one lives in a perspective that transcends the age and thus puts it in proportion. This both vindicates courage and safeguards against fanaticism." He then refers to Dietrich Bonhoeffer's term, that "all historical events are 'penultimate,' that their ultimate significance lies in a reality that transcends them and that transcends all the empirical coordinates of human existence" (*A Rumor of Angels: Modern Society and the Rediscovery of the Supernatural* [Garden City, N.Y.: Doubleday & Co., 1970], p. 96).

5. An example of such an effort is the long process within the National Council of the Churches of Christ which produced the policy statement *The Ethical Implications of Energy Production and Use.* While illustrative in certain respects of points we are making, in others it leaves much to be desired, especially as regards the need clearly to formulate the dynamic heart of our confessional heritage as a basis for addressing the question, but also as regards the need to draw on all relevant areas of expertise.

6. Ralph Abernathy, quoted from *The Boston Globe,* 5 April 1980.

7. Marie Augusta Neal, S.N.D.deN., *A Socio-Theology of Letting Go: The Role of a First World Church Facing Third World Peoples* (New York: Paulist Press, 1977), pp. 103–11.

8. Ibid., p. 105.

9. Ibid., p. 107.

10. Dietrich Bonhoeffer applies this text to modern life powerfully in "The Simplicity of the Carefree Life," in *The Cost of Discipleship,* 2d ed. (New York: Macmillan Co., 1959), pp. 154–61.

APPENDIX

1. This essay, previously published in the *Ecumenical Review* 27 (1975): 316–24, is used here by permission.

2. On the *'apiru* see G. Mendenhall, "The Hebrew Conquest of Palestine," *Biblical Archaeologist Reader,* vol. 3, Edward F. Campbell and David N. Freedman, eds. (New York: Doubleday & Co., 1970), pp. 100–120.

Indexes

SCRIPTURE REFERENCES

AUTHORS

SUBJECTS